SAMUEL PEPYS

and his world

SAM · PEPYS · CAR · ET · IAC · ANGL · REGIB · A · SECRETIS · ADMIRAL

J. G. Kneller pinx.

R. White sculp.

SAMUEL PEPYS

and his world

BY GEOFFREY TREASE

CHARLES SCRIBNER'S SONS

NEW YORK

1 3 5 7 9 11 13 15 17 19 I/C 20 18 16 14 12 10 8 6 4 2

Printed in Great Britain
Library of Congress Catalog Card Number 77–83234
ISBN 0–684–15512–5

London Bridge, dating from the twelfth century, was the only road-crossing of the Thames. Hence, partly, the importance of the London boatmen

'PEPYS . . . AND HIS WORLD.' Is there any name in history to which that comprehensive phrase can be attached with more genuine meaning? Pepys's world was small by modern standards, and one man with broad interests could touch it at many points. Pepys, with his insatiable curiosity, his sociable disposition and the opportunities provided by his office, was ideally equipped to 'know' the world in which he lived. In a single day he might be conferring with his sovereign, gossiping in a tavern with a ship's captain, a scholar or a merchant, watching a scientific demonstration at the Royal Society, and fondling an actress in the darkness of a coach. His life story mirrors Restoration England in all its exuberant variety.

Samuel Pepys was born on 23 February 1633 over his father's tailor's shop in Salisbury Court between Fleet Street and the Thames. He was thus from the start what he always remained, a Londoner.

His England was a green, slowly changing countryside, thinly populated by some five million inhabitants. Even in Salisbury Court, amid the tightly packed warren of the ancient city which the Great Fire of London was soon to sweep away, the fields were not far distant – could be glimpsed indeed from many a rooftop, such as the leads over the Navy Office in Seething Lane whereon, in his maturer years, Pepys loved to walk and talk and make music on sultry summer evenings.

His London was a city of comprehensible size, with which one bustling, indefatigable individual could fairly claim to be thoroughly familiar. Half a million people filled the narrow built-up area which hugged the curving north bank of the river from Westminster Abbey down to London Bridge and the Tower. In that three-mile stretch, whose waterfront panorama was so fortunately recorded for us by the Prague artist Wenceslaus Hollar, almost all the world of Pepys is encapsulated – palace and Parliament and playhouse, coffee house and tavern and fashionable church, Navy Office and Royal Exchange. And in that limited but richly varied territory, at one house or another, all his working life was based, though with sufficient excursions, both to other parts of the kingdom and to foreign countries, to provide him with a wider vision.

Ancestry   The Pepys family were not Londoners. They were rooted in the Cambridgeshire fens, and belonged to that sturdy, businesslike middle class which had emerged prominently in Tudor England. Before the dissolution of the monasteries they had for generations served as bailiffs to Crowland Abbey. Thereafter they had prospered as lawyers and country squires. Some, however, had gravitated to the capital and one of these was John Pepys. After serving his apprenticeship to a London tailor he had set up in business in Salisbury Court. He was among the humbler members of the family and he did not enhance his status by marrying a washmaid, Margaret Kite, whose brother was a butcher in Whitechapel.

Samuel was the fifth of their eleven children, but child mortality was high, and soon he ranked as eldest. Only two brothers, Tom and John, and one sister, Paulina or 'Pall', attained maturity. Samuel grew up, like most people of his century, with a sharp awareness of Death lurking round the corner, but it never, for more than brief moments, damped down his ebullience.

The home atmosphere was in general Puritan. This was the sober mercantile London with which Shakespeare and the raffish players had waged continual war, the London which, in the actual war now fast approaching, would ensure the eventual victory of Parliament over the King. But Pepys did not spend his early years in a bigoted or gloomy household. His father played the bass viol, and the boy quickly imbibed that love of music which later gave him such consolation and delight. Similarly, he acquired his appetite for the theatre, slipping off whenever he could to the Red Bull at Clerkenwell, where particularly robust and gory melodramas were put on. He must have been no more than nine, perhaps younger, for the summer of 1642 brought the Civil War and the closing of all theatres.

Round about this time he was sent away to live with relatives in the country. This move was probably due to his health, and the appalling series of recent deaths among his little brothers and sisters – in 1637, 1638, 1640 (two) and 1641 – rather than to the political upheaval. He was an ailing child. 'I remember not my life without the pain of the stone in the kidneys,' he wrote later, 'till I was about

6

The city of Pepys's childhood: a map published about 1645. Ringed: Salisbury Court, to the west, and Seething Lane, near the Tower. (*Below*) The busy waterfront of seventeenth-century London, with the green slopes of Highgate visible in the distance

The Tower and eastern end of London, seen from Southwark. (*Below*) The open fields at Islington where Pepys recalled playing, as a child, with his bow and arrows

The house at Brampton where Pepys stayed as a boy with his uncle Robert

twenty years of age.' Once before he had been sent with Tom to board for a while with an old nurse, Goody Lawrence, in the fresh air of Kingsland just outside the city. One of his earliest recollections was of rambling through those open fields near Islington and shooting with his miniature bow and arrows. Now he went further, to stay with his uncle Robert Pepys at Brampton, near Huntingdon and not so many miles from his Cambridgeshire relatives.

Huntingdon was a small market town, hardly more than a single long street, but it contained a grammar school, where Oliver Cromwell himself had received his education some thirty years earlier. More recently, and more relevantly to Samuel Pepys's future, it had been attended by his own kinsman, Edward Montagu or (to adopt his own spelling) Mountagu. It was doubtless on his recommendation that the small boy from London was sent to the school for the next two or three years.

Huntingdon

Mountagu was to play an important role in Pepys's later life. It cannot be said that without him there would have been no *Diary*, but it is likely that without him Pepys would never have been in a position to make some of its most interesting entries, especially his eye-witness accounts of critical moments in history.

Mountagu

Mountagu was his first cousin once removed, his elder by seven and a half years, though at this age the gap between them must have seemed infinite. For in 1643,

9

Edward Mountagu, Pepys's cousin
and consistent patron,
usually referred to as 'my Lord'

when the ten-year-old Pepys was learning his Latin declensions, the eighteen-year-old Mountagu – in spite of a Royalist father – was raising his own Parliamentary regiment, with which he soon distinguished himself at Marston Moor and Naseby. It is not surprising that Pepys, with such a dashing cousin to look up to, should be confirmed in the political sympathies already implanted in him by his London childhood.

About 1645, the Naseby year, Pepys returned to his parents in Salisbury Court *St Paul's School* and was admitted to St Paul's School, a few minutes' walk away, beyond the Fleet River and up Ludgate Hill, where the old massively towered church brooded over its graveyard and the rows of booksellers.

Pepys was happy at school. He was by nature a conformist, he enjoyed learning, and excelling, and his readiness to find interest in all things gave him, more than the average boy, a defence against the boredom of a rigid seventeenth-century education.

The form of that education, and his general approval of it, may be fairly deduced from what he wrote in later years. On 4 February 1663 he revisited his old school and heard the boys' speeches, 'and they were just as schoolboys' used to be, of the seven liberal sciences; but I think not so good as ours were in our time.' Later in the day he went back 'to see the head forms posed in Latin, Greek, and Hebrew, but I think they did not answer in any so well as we did, only in geography they did pretty well.'

It is significant that he remained on excellent terms with his old headmaster. On 23 December 1661 he recorded a happy encounter at his bookseller's with Dr Samuel Cromleholme, who was a bibliophil like himself, and the second master, Nathaniel Bull. He took them both to the Star tavern 'and there we sat and talked; and I had great pleasure in their company.' Before they parted, Pepys 'did offer to give the school what book he would choose of five pounds', a promise which he fulfilled by presenting four volumes of Stephanus's *Thesaurus Graecae Linguae*, the finest Greek lexicon then available.

No less welcome to Pepys were the occasional encounters with his old school-fellows, even though – as can happen in such cases – they evoked embarrassing reminiscences. Thus, on 1 November 1660, he found himself at a dinner party with another Old Pauline named Christmas, now 'a deadly drinker' and 'grown exceeding fat'. Pepys by this date had firmly hitched his rising star to the wagon of the restored Charles II. It was unfortunate when Christmas 'did remember that I was a great roundhead when I was a boy, and I was much afeared that he would have remembered the words that I said the day that the King was beheaded (that were I to preach upon him, my text would be: "The memory of the wicked shall rot"); but I found afterward that he did go away from school before that time.'

St Paul's School rebuilt to its old design after the Fire. Pepys always kept up a close connection with his old school

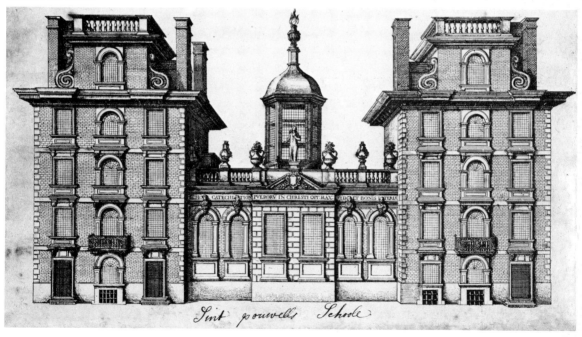

The trial of Charles I: Pepys's cousin Mountagu disapproved and for some time quitted public life.
(*Below*) The King's execution, witnessed by Pepys as a schoolboy with enthusiastic
Roundhead sympathies

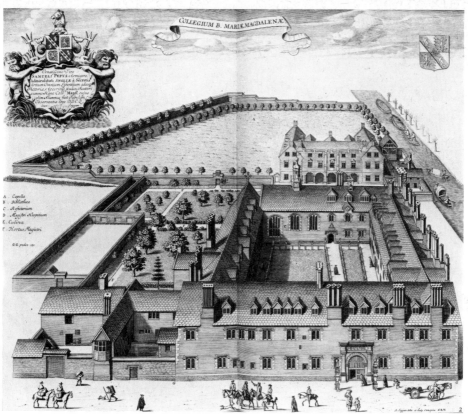

Magdalene College, Cambridge, scene of three happy years, 1650-3

As a boy, still not sixteen, Pepys had squeezed into the throng to witness the grim pageantry of the King's execution. At that time, clearly, he had felt no qualms about its justice. With his admired cousin, Mountagu, it had been different. Though much favoured by Cromwell as one of his most promising young officers, Mountagu had made no secret of his disapproval and had dropped out of political life for five years. Thus he escaped the stigma of regicide, which in 1660 proved most fortunate for him and, indirectly, for that erstwhile 'great roundhead', his cousin Sam.

In 1650 Pepys went to Cambridge, a step made possible for one in such humble circumstances only by the award of a grant from the Mercers' Company. He was originally put down for Trinity Hall, where another of his numerous cousins was a Fellow, but he transferred to Magdalene College and went into residence there on 5 March, a week or two after his eighteenth birthday.

Cambridge

The Cambridge of those days was a small place. A mere few hundred students were distributed among some sixteen colleges, each of which therefore formed a compact society, except for those inequalities of station which Pepys felt as keenly as any. Though his room-mate, Robert Sawyer, rose to be Attorney-General, few of his Cambridge intimates achieved success comparable with his own – a fact he subsequently noted with some complacency. His more distinguished contemporaries at the university, he frankly acknowledged, were 'then (God knows) much above me'. His tutor, Samuel Morland, knew Mountagu and eventually achieved a knighthood. More than thirty years after those Cambridge days, an ineffectual and bankrupt inventor of naval pumps, gun-carriages and other devices, he proved rather an embarrassment to his good-natured former pupil, who nevertheless gave what help he could.

Shorthand   During those three years at Magdalene, Pepys studied with reasonable diligence and was awarded college scholarships. Along with his Latin and mathematics he almost certainly learnt at this time, as a voluntary task, the shorthand he found so useful afterwards not only for the *Diary* but on countless other occasions in his public business. Shelton's *Tachygraphy* had been published by the Cambridge University Press and was much approved by scholars, including Edward Rainbowe, who was Master of Magdalene at the time of Pepys's arrival. Shorthand became yet another of that youth's life-long interests. Over the next forty years he collected thirty-two textbooks and pamphlets on the subject, some rare and one unique, and one dating from the time of the Spanish Armada.

Cambridge from the west, seen across the unenclosed fields. Pepys liked to walk with his friends in the surrounding countryside

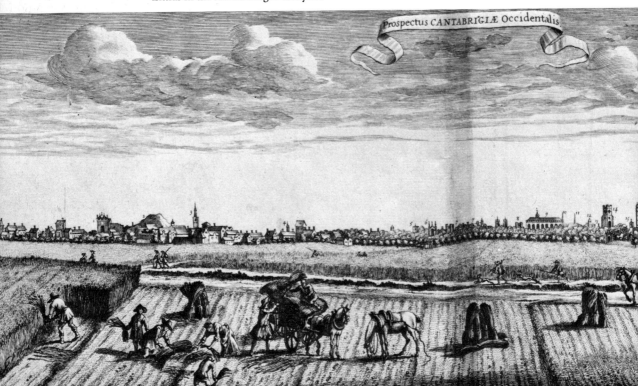

Prospectus CANTABRIGIÆ Occidentalis

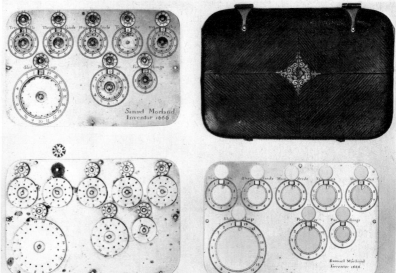

Samuel Morland, Pepys's Cambridge tutor, an ingenious opportunist who later tried his hand at political intrigue and technical inventions. (*Right*) Calculating machine – typical of Morland's inventions and also of the general experimental spirit of the period. (*Below*) How Pepys learnt shorthand. His copy of Shelton's *Tachygraphy*, with his own annotations

They muſt, and they are only four, namely, *Ch ſh th wh*, which you ſhall find altogether at the end of the Copy which have peculiar markes without relation to the letters.

First, becauſe they cannot be conveniently expreſſed by their proper characters in ſo ſhort a roome.

Secondly, being very frequently uſed, I thought good to fit them with characters that might ſoone be diſpatched

C H A P. I V.
Concerning the Vowels places.

Queſt. 10 I Am ſatisfyed concerning the letters, and double Conſonants ; how ſhall I underſtand the next rule, concerning the vowels places.

Anſwer. The directions for knowing each vowels place ſet downe in Chapter 4. are ſufficient for the meaneſt capacity to underſtand. The place of each vowell muſt perfectly be remembred ; that as ſoone as you thinke of that vowell you may know where the place of it is. As for example, if the vowell be *A*, the place of it is juſt over the head of any

any letter. *E*, even with the upper part of the letter toward the right hand. *I*, juſt againſt the middeſt of the letter. *O*, even with the lower part of it. *V*, juſt under the letter about which it is to be placed.

Queſt. 11 But I have ſeen in ſome Bookes of Short-writing, ſome of the vowels placed behind, and ſome before, were it not better to place them ſo, then to ſet them all upon one ſide ?

Anſw. No, thoſe that have ſo placed the vowels have found it no ſmall hinderance to their ſpeed in writing, and to the reading of what hath beene ſo written, And it is eaſie for any to underſtand, that when the vowels are ſo placed, as that ſtill the hand is moving forward, it muſt needs be a helpe to celerity.

C H A P. V.
Concerning the uſe of the Vowels.

Queſt. 12 YOu have given ſufficient direction concerning the placing of the vowels : but in the 5. Chapter, concerning the uſe of the vowels and their places, though there be ſome directions and examples, yet I doe not well underſtand it, therefore I deſire ſome

Cromwell cuts down the royal oak, along with the Bible, Magna Carta and British liberties: a cartoon put out by his political opponents after the King's execution in 1649 ▶

Rear court of Magdalene, showing the frontage of what is now the Pepys Library

Such private hobbies never prevented him from enjoying himself with the crowd. At Cambridge he took country walks with his friends, drank deep in the local taverns and learnt to sing bawdy songs like *Full Forty Times Over*. Once Morland had to admonish him solemnly, before the assembled Fellows, for being scandalously drunk the night before. Even under the Commonwealth, university men could not be turned into Puritans. Another of Pepys's weaknesses made itself apparent at this time, his susceptibility to women. Some youthful infatuation, the record of which is now untraceable, inspired him to dash off a play, which he entitled *Love A Cheat*. Turning up the manuscript in later years, he hastily burnt it.

Illness　　A weakness of quite another kind developed while he was at Cambridge. On a hot day in the summer of 1653 he joined a party of young men and walked out to Aristotle's Well, where they all drank liberally of the icy spring water before turning back to college. The sequel, for Pepys, was several days of agony and alarm. A stone had passed from the kidney to the bladder, where it gave him increasing trouble over the next few years. It was a complaint from which both his mother and his brother John afterwards suffered.

Except for this alarming episode, and the brooding anxiety it left behind, Cambridge, like his schooldays, left mainly agreeable memories. He always retained a strong affection for his college. In 1677 he was one of the subscribers towards the new buildings which now, fittingly, house the Pepys Library, preserving the books, papers and other effects he bequeathed to Magdalene at his death.

16

He took his B.A. degree in March 1654, and went home to Salisbury Court. What he did for the next year or so is obscure: in later times he was reticent on the subject. Very possibly he helped his father in some humble capacity. He was most likely marking time, hoping for help from his cousin Mountagu, who had just made his peace with Cromwell and returned to public life. Mountagu had a seat on the Council of State, a post as Treasury Commissioner, and a lodging in the vast, rambling palace of Whitehall, where the Lord Protector had now been installed with quasi-regal splendour. Mountagu, still only twenty-eight, seemed likely to go far, and with luck Pepys might be drawn along at his coat-tails.

Mountagu, for his part, could use a bright young relative. Pepys's loyalty was dependable: his discretion had to be proved. Mountagu tested it by degrees. He used Pepys first as a sort of personal assistant – apart from his official appointments he had his country estate at Hinchingbrooke – and then, when opportunity came, found him employment in the public service. It was a long time before he took his cousin fully into his confidence. It was not, indeed, until 7 November 1660, when the gamble of Restoration year had come off, that Pepys could write, marvelling at the revelations just made to him: 'I do from this raise an opinion of him to be one of the most secret men in the world – which I was not so convinced of before.'

Five years earlier, England's future and Pepys's had worn a very different appearance. Cromwell looked firmly established in the seat of power: Pepys, the penniless young graduate, was anything but established. To cap everything, before his cousin had had time to do much for him, he fell passionately in love and rashly got married. The church ceremony was on 10 October 1655 but the legal formalities before a magistrate, as required by the new Commonwealth law, did not take place until 1 December.

Marriage

Elizabeth St Michel was a lovely, vivacious fifteen-year-old, the daughter of a penniless French Protestant and his Anglo-Irish wife. She was warmly affectionate, jealous – often with good reason – and as undomesticated as she was unintellectual. It was more the contrast in their natures than the age-gap, a mere seven years, that at times made them behave like hectoring schoolmaster and petulant pupil.

Pepys tried to improve her mind by constantly reading to her, but what she really enjoyed was some long, sentimental French romance. This he might have accepted, but it was embarrassing when she insisted on retailing the plots to a helpless audience. 'I find my wife troubled,' runs the *Diary* entry for 12 May 1666, 'at my checking her last night in the coach, in her long stories out of Grand Cyrus, which she would tell, though nothing to the purpose, nor in any good manner.'

Poor Elizabeth could not spell, even by the somewhat free-and-easy standards of the time. On 31 January 1663 Pepys came in after a hard day at the office and a 'not very good' dinner, 'only a rabbit not half roasted, which made me angry with my wife', and set to checking two socially important letters she had written (one to Mountagu's wife) which 'were so falsely spelt that I was ashamed of them, and took occasion to fall out about them . . . and so she wrote none, at which, however, I was sorry . . .'.

Elizabeth's carelessness and untidiness were a constant irritation, for, wrote Pepys, 'my delight is in the neatness of everything, and so cannot be pleased with anything unless it be very neat.' On 6 January 1663 he was 'somewhat vexed at my wife's neglect in leaving of her scarf, waistcoat, and night-dressings in the coach today that brought us from Westminster, though,' he added with that honesty which makes the *Diary* so endearing, 'I confess, she did give them to me to look after, yet it was her fault not to see that I did take them out of the coach. I believe it might be as good as twentyfive shillings loss or thereabouts.' Worse was to follow. Three weeks later Elizabeth came home in tears. She had bought herself a new waistcoat in Cheapside and as she was returning with it in a coach 'a man asked her whether that was the way to the Tower; and while she was answering him, another, on the other side, snatched away her bundle out of her lap, and could not be recovered, but ran away with it, which vexes me cruelly, but it cannot be helped.'

Meals might go wrong and other household crises occur, but there is plenty of evidence in the *Diary* that the girl did her best to please. 'My poor wife rose by 5 o'clock in the morning, before day' – this was January – 'and went to market and bought fowls and many other things for dinner. . . .' They were giving an

Elizabeth, who, as a vivacious
fifteen-year-old, had
become Mrs Pepys in 1655

important party and Pepys was highly satisfied with 'our management of the day'. On other occasions, also in January, 'my wife was making of her tarts and larding of her pullets until 11 a-clock', and 'I sat up till the bellman came by with his bell, just under my window as I was writing of this very line, and cried, "Past one of the clock, and a cold, frosty, windy morning." I then went to bed and left my wife and the maid a-washing still.' Wash-day was a formidable operation which luckily came only once a month.

For all their sulks and squabbles they were an affectionate couple. Pepys was proud of his wife's beauty and loved to note how she outshone other women at social gatherings. Like many a conventional husband, however, he inveighed against new fashions that he considered unnatural – though not with any consistency. When she put on black patches he thought her 'very pretty', but when she assumed 'light-coloured locks, quite white almost,' while he admitted that these too made her 'very pretty', he was vexed, although 'like a fool I helped her the other night to buy them'. This continued to be a bone of contention between them. A year later, 11 May 1667, the *Diary* records: 'My wife being dressed this day in fair hair did make me so mad, that I spoke not one word to her, though I was ready to burst with anger.' He found words when they were alone together in the coach on the way home, when he voiced his indignation to her 'for her white locks, swearing

The Maidens Resolution;

OR,

An ANSVVER to the ADVICE against

TOP-KNOTS.

Tune of, *Te Ladies of London.*   *This may be Printed,* R. P.

WHat is the matter you make such ado,
    come tell us we now do require?
Must we young Damsels be ruled by you,
    concerning our Youthful Attire?
Are we not brisk and just in our prime,
    then what is the cause we should spare it?
Though we wear Top-Knots, I hope 'tis no Crime,
    for if we win Gold we will wear it.

As for the Women of Old, which you say,
    might learn us a modest Behaviour,
They, I declare, was as proud in their way,
    as we in our flourishing Favour:

Had they not Gold and other rich Stuff?
    to us they were no ways inferior,
She was no Woman that had not a Ruff,
    the which was a thousand times dearer.

Draggel-tayl'd Girls, you are pleased to call
    the Country Damsels at pleasure,
Are they not often the best of us all
    in London, well furnisht with Treasure?
Is not the best of Citizens Wives,
    from Country-Cities descended?
Here they do flourish and lead happy lives,
    then why should you Fools be offended?

Elizabeth and Samuel had
many a quarrel over fashions
in hair and dress. This ballad
comes from his own collection

Elizabeth's extravagant
shopping forays upset her
husband. Hollar's picture of
muffs, lace, mask, fan and
other fripperies might have
moved him to vehement
comment *(below)*

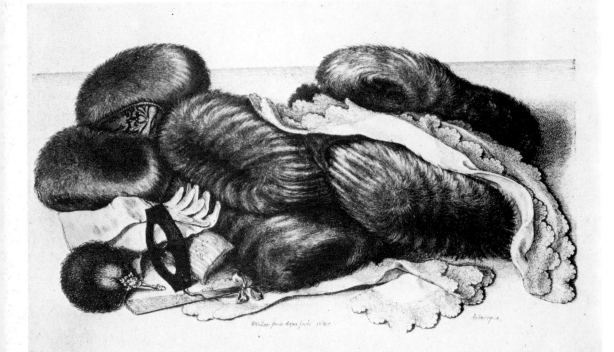

A typical riverside landing place at Whitehall. The seventeenth-century Thames had shelving banks of tidal mud, not the granite embankments of today

several times, which I pray God forgive me for, and bending my fist, that I would not endure it. She, poor wretch, was surprised with it, and made me no answer all the way home; but there we parted, and I to the office late, and then home, and without supper to bed, vexed.'

Bed, unfortunately, was not always the solvent of their disagreements. Elizabeth suffered from irregular and painful periods, and also from local swellings which sometimes inhibited their love-making. In 1660 the *Diary* sadly recorded 'her old pain in the lip of her *chose*, which she had when we were first married.' In due course this trouble seems to have disappeared, but the physical difficulties of those early years had not helped the smooth development of their marriage.

Their first home was an apartment in the Palace of Whitehall, for in January *Whitehall home* 1656, within a month or two of the wedding, Mountagu was made joint commander, with the famous Admiral Blake, of the English battle fleet then mustering for the war with Spain. Mountagu needed a reliable representative to take care of his affairs in London while he was at sea. This was Pepys's first real opportunity, and he rose to it. With his fifteen-year-old bride he took up his allotted quarters in a small turret near the great gateway.

21

All that survives today of Whitehall Palace: Inigo Jones's banqueting hall with its Rubens ceiling

Today only Inigo Jones's banqueting hall, with its Rubens ceiling, recalls the palace which was then by far the largest in Europe. Whitehall was not, of course, a single building. It was an agglomeration, a precinct, a maze of architectural units interwoven with galleries, courtyards and gardens, sprawling over twenty-three acres. Even the Vatican covered less than fourteen, Versailles only seven. Important foreign visitors marvelled, and in private sneered, for of its two thousand rooms scarcely one was really comfortable, and many lacked even a door. There were mountainous fires of coal and logs, and they were needed. In this draughty labyrinth Cromwell kept his state, attended by red-coated troopers and black-suited gentle-men with silver trimmings. Near by, in homelier but doubtless more cheerful fashion, the young Mr and Mrs Pepys began their married life.

As his cousin's agent Pepys had many responsibilities and only modest remunera-tion. While Mountagu was on the high seas he had to deal with correspondence and execute all kinds of commissions for him. He had to control, as best he could, the small domestic staff left in Mountagu's lodgings, and he had to deal with his opposite numbers on the country estate at Hinchingbrooke, the agent and the steward, and keep on the right side of Mountagu's elder sister and the rest of the family. Even shopping fell within his province – even, indeed, the purchase of caps for Mountagu's little girls. Meanwhile he and Elizabeth lived in one room in the turret, she making the fire and washing his linen in a century when it was hard to keep up one's dignity without employing servants. But soon virtue was rewarded. Through personal influence, probably of Mountagu, who had been a Treasury Commissioner since August 1654 – influence was needed for any employment – he became clerk to one of the four Tellers of the Exchequer, the strict and for-bidding George Downing, whose name lives on in the famous side-street in modern Whitehall. It was a personal rather than a government post, but it put Pepys's foot on the right ladder. He was able to see how public administration was carried on. He picked up knowledge and friends of future usefulness.

Whether he would have any future, however – a physical existence, let alone a career – looked highly problematical at the beginning of 1658.

The symptoms which had troubled him since childhood, and then culminated *Operation* in the short but agonizing illness at Cambridge, were recurring with more and more insistency. His father introduced him to Thomas Hollier, a surgeon at St Thomas's Hospital who specialized in lithotomy, or 'cutting for the stone', one of the few serious operations then feasible and, even so, very much a kill-or-cure affair. Pepys was a timid, apprehensive man, on occasions comical in his cowardice but on others capable of extraordinary courage. He agreed to the operation.

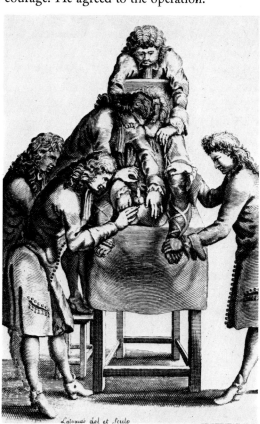

Surgery before anaesthetics:
an all-too-vivid impression,
by a French artist, of a
patient being 'cut for the stone'

Latouuie del et sculo

The necessary incision was in those days made from below, through the perineum. An expert surgeon like William Cheselden, two generations later, is said to have been able to perform the operation in a minute. His record was fifty-four seconds. Even if Hollier was equally swift, a minute in that pre-anaesthetic century must have been a minute too long, while the preceding agonies of anticipation are immeasurable. The only mild alleviation offered to Pepys was a concoction of rose water, white of egg, liquorice and other ingredients, prescribed by Dr Moleyns of St Bartholomew's.

He underwent his ordeal on 26 March. As neither his own Whitehall room nor his parents' home was spacious enough, a relative in Salisbury Court, Mrs Turner, made her house available. It was not merely that the surgeon and his assistants needed elbow room – all the family had to crowd in, ready for what might develop, at a moment's notice, into a death-bed scene. In the event it did not. Hollier did his work deftly, and, fortunately for Pepys and posterity, no infection followed. The stone, which Pepys kept and often displayed, weighed two ounces. He had good reason for celebrating the anniversary in later years with a handsome thanksgiving dinner to his friends, not forgetting Mrs Turner. The operation proved a complete success. Only, as it has been suggested by a modern expert, it possibly did some injury to his genito-urinary system which may explain some of his sexual excitability, his prurience in a literal sense. This, taken in conjunction with the physical discomfort which inclined his wife the other way, contributed to their marital problems and provoked him to misbehaviour.

Axe Yard One way and another, 1658 was a memorable year for him. During that summer, recovered from his operation, he was able to establish Elizabeth in a real home of her own, a modest little house in Axe Yard, close to what is now Horse Guards Parade. He could even give her a maid, a good-natured, gentle but occasionally high-spirited girl named Jane Birch. She was paid three pounds a year. Pepys's own salary from George Downing was only fifty.

It was a bad summer. A late spring was followed by weeks of bitter north winds, bringing icy hailstorms in June. On 30 August, four days after Jane had taken up her duties, England was struck by the most violent storm in living memory. Church steeples and chimneys toppled, countless ships at sea capsized and sank. That same evening Cromwell, rousing himself from a feverish sleep, confided to *Death of Cromwell* the Secretary of State, John Thurloe, that he wished his son Richard to succeed him as Lord Protector. Four days later, on 3 September, he died.

The succession was effected smoothly. 'There is not a dog that wags his tongue,' wrote the astute Thurloe, 'so great a calm are we in.' But the mild, unpolitical Richard, though proclaimed without opposition, was not the man to cope with the problems of the time. The air smelt of coming change. Pepys, ears cocked to the gossip of Whitehall, was as concerned as any to know what would happen now.

Servants were essential in the humblest gentleman's home. The mistress – and often the master –
expected a degree of personal service reserved only for the very few today

Dissensions broke out in the new year, when Richard Cromwell summoned a
fresh Parliament. The army generals despised him because he was not one of them,
and they formed a council in opposition. Trouble was brewing when, in March,
Mountagu was dispatched with a fleet to the Baltic, where the new Lord Protector
wished him to mediate between Sweden and Denmark. Within a few weeks the
army, in open revolt, had forced Richard to dissolve his Parliament. Clearly his
own fall could not be long delayed.

Pepys, watching his patron's interests closely, now made his first brief entry upon
the stage of history. The ketch *Hind* was sailing with dispatches for the admiral.
Pepys seized the chance to make a confidential report in person and took passage
in her, thus gaining his first, and fortunately agreeable experience of the sea. On
26 May he clambered aboard his cousin's flagship. Only the day before, the army
council had deposed Richard Cromwell and tossed him contemptuously into the
harmless oblivion of private life, where he survived for another fifty-three years.

Pepys's taste of naval life was brief. On the morrow he was homeward bound in
the *Hind*, wondering very much how his cousin would conduct himself in this
uncertain situation.

Voyage to Baltic

In fact, though Pepys did not learn of it until much later, the enigmatic Mountagu was already in secret correspondence with the future Charles II, then an impecunious twenty-nine-year-old exile, hovering hopefully in France. Mountagu was essentially a moderate – a loyal Cromwellian, who had none the less recoiled from extreme measures against Charles I and who never forgot the favours shown to his own father by James I. In religion, he later revealed himself to Pepys, he was 'wholly sceptical, as well as I. . . . He likes uniformity and form of prayer.' By the same token, in politics – not easy at that time to separate from religion – he was a pragmatist who valued order and stability above everything else.

He was not alone in feeling that the restoration of the monarchy, though not an ideal solution, was the only way to avert anarchy. The generals, on dissolving Richard Cromwell's Parliament, had brought back the fifty surviving members of the Long Parliament originally elected in 1640, a residue disrespectfully known as the Rump. Mountagu, still anchored in the Baltic, received increasingly dis-tasteful dispatches from this new regime. When, in August, there was an abortive royalist rising, Mountagu – by a coincidence which took some explaining – disregarded his instructions and sailed home at the head of his fleet, arriving too late, however, to affect the outcome either way. After some rather chilly interviews in London he retired to Hinchingbrooke and lay low on his country estate. That autumn Pepys became in an even fuller sense his London agent, apprising him of the way the political undercurrents flowed.

Diary begun   Though it was hardly 'bliss . . . in that dawn to be alive', it was undeniably interesting, and as 1659 drew to a close, with the virtual certainty of epoch-making events about to occur, the methodical young man resolved to begin 1660 with a journal. He bought an octavo notebook, ruled margins in red ink, and, using Shelton's shorthand to protect political and private indiscretions alike from other eyes, wrote the introductory summary:

'Blessed be God, at the end of the last year I was in very good health, without any sense of my old pain but upon taking cold.

'I lived in Axe-yard, having my wife and servant Jane, and no more in family than us three.

'My wife, after the absence of her terms for seven weeks, gave me hopes of her being with child, but on the last day of the year she hath them again. The condition of the State was thus. *Viz.* the Rump, after being disturbed by my Lord Lambert, was lately returned to sit again. The officers of the army all forced to yield. Lawson lies still in the River and Monck is with his army in Scotland. . . .'

Even as Pepys inscribed those words in his neat shorthand characters, Monck and his soldiers were beginning the march southwards which was to play so decisive a part in the Restoration. Day by day, throughout the first months of 1660, the *Diary* vividly chronicles the course of events – the political manœuvres, Monck's

General John Lambert, who 'disturbed' the Rump Parliament and helped to overthrow Richard Cromwell. (*Right*) 'The Burning of the Rump': the London butchers played a leading part in the hilarious political demonstrations against the old Parliament

taking over of Whitehall Palace, talk in the coffee houses, unpaid and mutinous soldiers demonstrating in the streets 'for a free Parliament and money', and the wild scenes of rejoicing when Monck, the man of the moment, who alone wielded effective power, declared himself in favour of new elections. Pepys describes how he walked home at ten o'clock that night, with 'Bow bells and all the bells in all the churches . . . a-ringing'. In the Strand he counted thirty-one bonfires in view at the same time. Rumps were being paraded on sticks in symbolic derision of the old Parliament, and the butchers, gathered where the maypole had always stood in the good old days, 'rang a peal with their knives' as the rump was solemnly consigned to the flames. The whole thing 'was past imagination, both the greatness and the suddenness of it. At one end of the street, you would think there was a whole lane of fire. . . .' When he reached home, he could not bear to let Elizabeth miss all the excitement, so out they went into the February night and walked through the noisy streets as far as the Exchange and back. Interspersed with the descriptions of these stirring national events are all the homelier personal trivia which make the *Diary*

27

General George Monck, prime mover in Charles II's restoration, for which he was created Duke of Albemarle. This portrait, by the famous miniaturist Samuel Cooper, dates from about 1670. (*Right*) Oliver Cromwell's son and brief successor, deposed by the Army in 1659

such a treasure-house of social history, like the gift of the live turkey which Elizabeth had to kill, herself, the maid being too squeamish ever to kill anything. The *Diary* does not mention whether Pepys volunteered.

There was open talk of the King's return, now, but everything remained uncertain. Some preferred Monck, and there were still those who pressed the name of Richard Cromwell. Until a new Parliament could be elected no decision was possible. Many awkward questions remained unanswered. Even those who wished the King 'to enjoy his own again' did not interpret the phrase too exactly, for it was impossible to go back to 1642 – it meant unscrambling too many eggs. There must be guarantees before Charles could be invited to wear his father's crown.

Mountagu reappeared in London, diplomatic, disclosing nothing of his own year-long secret correspondence with the King. The outgoing Parliament appointed him one of the two 'generals at sea'. As the other was Monck, who had plenty to do on land with the army, this gave Mountagu immediate control of the fleet.

A few days later he had a serious talk with Pepys about his future, advising him to look round for 'some good place' and promising to use all his influence to help. Then, as they walked together in the Whitehall garden, he came out with his own proposition. He asked 'whether I could without too much inconvenience go to sea as his Secretary, and bade me think of it.'

Pepys thought about it for three days, and lost a good deal of sleep worrying over so momentous a decision. He did not tell Elizabeth until it was made. She was only nineteen, and (whether because of her youth and beauty or of the disturbed political situation, the *Diary* does not say) he was not going to leave her with only the maid's companionship in the little house in Axe Yard. He had an anxious consultation with his father in the cutting-room at his shop. Mr Pepys senior suggested that she might go and board with a friendly family, the Bowyers, in Buckinghamshire. Pepys thought this an excellent notion and, rather late in the day, broke the news to Elizabeth of what he had decided for both of them. She was 'much troubled' and there was 'some dispute', but she finally agreed. The next two weeks were filled with feverish preparations for departure, which included Elizabeth's making caps for him, 'the wench' completing a knitted pair of stockings, and Pepys drawing up his will in case he never returned. Elizabeth was left 'all that I have in the world but my books'. His brother John was to have these – they would not be of much use to Elizabeth, except the French ones, which he did assign to her as the only ones likely to appeal.

Bad weather delayed his embarkation but at last, on 23 March, he was able to take a hackney coach down to the Tower, where Mountagu ('my Lord', as he is normally referred to in the *Diary*) stepped into the Admiral's barge and Pepys followed in the next boat, a dignified figure despite his very modest stature of five foot six, punctiliously dressed and complete with new rapier. Pepys basked in the glory reflected from his cousin, when, as my Lord came aboard his temporary flagship, the *Swiftsure*, all the anchored frigates fired their cannon in salute. Going below, Pepys was gratified to find that he had been given the best cabin of all those allotted to my Lord's staff. It seemed as if he had, in another sense, arrived. Two days later he felt the thrill of picking up a letter to himself, personally addressed by the Secretary to the Admiralty, with the addition of *'Esqr.'* This coveted abbreviation conferred a status above that of mere 'Gentleman'.

The Tower and its wharf, where Pepys stepped out of his hackney coach and into a naval barge on 23 March 1660: the first step in the long career that took him to the highest post in the Admiralty

Charles, though chronically short of money, passed his years of exile as agreeably as he could.
The young man seated is his brother Henry, Duke of Gloucester, who died unmarried within
a few months of the Restoration

Reading and writing letters, along with orders, lists and the like, kept him in his
cabin for most of those early days aboard. The ships lay in the river for another week
or two. There was much to be done. In any case the fleet could not move until a new
Parliament had met and decided – what more and more people now looked forward
to as the best solution – that the King be fetched home from Holland, where he now
was. Mountagu kept his own counsel, seemingly the obedient servant of the
nation. But Pepys noticed that, along with all the comings and goings natural in a
fleet being fitted out for a voyage, passes were required for various individuals
crossing backwards and forwards to the Continent on unspecified errands.

He was enjoying himself immensely. Despite some occasional queasiness, he
took to the life afloat. When there was work to do, he worked diligently, sometimes
writing until midnight, and then back at his table at three o'clock in the morning.
But the work came in waves. There were agreeable lulls for long talks, music, and
ninepins, a game at which he mostly seemed to lose a few shillings, thereby no
doubt enhancing his reputation as a thoroughly good fellow. All the senior officers
and other notables treated him with respect. One evening, when he was celebrating
as best he could the anniversary of his operation, the captain himself came to his
cabin 'and sat drinking a bottle of wine till 11 a⁄clock at night, which is a kindness
he doth not usually do to the greatest officer in the ship.'

After a few days my Lord transferred himself, his twelve-year-old son Edward, and his entourage to his old flagship, the *Naseby*, in the circumstances an unfortunate name. At noon on 5 April, having previously moved down-river in short stages, they weighed anchor and crept out from the widening jaws of the Thames estuary towards the open sea. For more than a month longer, however, they had to hang about off the coast of Kent until all the political formalities in London could achieve their foregone conclusions. Gentlemen who dined aboard, coming fresh from London, told how the royal arms were reappearing openly in churches and private houses, and how the Mercers Company had commissioned a statue of the late King, ready to set up in the Exchange.

On 1 May the King's letter from Holland, the famous 'Declaration of Breda', was read to both Houses of Parliament, which forthwith voted for his restoration. Pepys was by then at Deal, where the joyful news arrived next day, and the 'seamen, as many as have money or credit for drink, did do nothing else this evening'. The next morning Mountagu called a council of war in his state-room to discuss the terms Charles had proposed, and Parliament already accepted, for his return. Mountagu took the wise precaution, before the captains came aboard, of dictating to Pepys the wording of the loyal resolution he wished them to pass. 'Resolved (*nemine contradicente*),' it ran, 'that the Commanders and Officers of the Fleet do receive the gracious Declaration of his Majesty . . .', and went on to express 'their exact loyalty and duty' to him. Pepys rose to his new responsibilities as though born to them. He read out the King's Declaration and letter addressed to the fleet, and then, while the captains debated them, went through a convincing pretence of setting down a consensus of their views. Mountagu's draft resolution was then put. 'Not one man seemed to say no to it,' Pepys recorded that night, 'though I am confident many in their hearts were against it.' He had learnt his first lesson in the steering of a conference.

Mountagu could be sure now that in his young cousin he had found a treasure, not merely loyal and hardworking but also able and astute. That evening – after Pepys had spent an exciting day being rowed from vessel to vessel with his proclamation, being everywhere received with 'respect and honour' – my Lord took him more fully into his confidence, showing him the private letters he had received from the King and his brother, the Duke of York, 'in such familiar style as to their common friend, with all kindness imaginable'. The next day, clearly not regretting the disclosures of the night before, Mountagu showed Pepys a reply he was about to send off to Charles, 'to see whether I could find any slips in it or no'.

Before that, Pepys had been busy sending off letters with copies of the resolution passed by the council of war. He took care in every case to append his own name, so that 'if it should come in print, my name may be at it'. He was learning fast.

It was another week before, on 12 May, 'my Lord did give order for weighing

His Majesties Letter to the Generals of the Navy at Sea. Charles Rex.

Rusty and well-beloved, We greet you well: It is no small comfort to us, after so many great troubles and miseries, which the whole Nation hath goaned under; and after so great Revolutions which have still increased those miseries, to hear that the Fleet and Ships which are the Wall of the Kingdom, are put under the Command of two Persons so well disposed and concerned in the peace and happiness of the Kingdom, as we believe you to be; and that the Officers and Seamen under your command, are more inclined to return to their duty to us, and put a period to the distempers and distractions which have so impoverished and dishonoured the Nation, then to widen the breach, and raise their fortunes by rapine and violence; which gives us great encouragement and hope, That God Almighty will heal the wounds by the same Plaister that made the Flesh raw; that he will proceed in the same method in pouring his blessings upon us, which he was pleased to use when he began to afflict us; and that the manifestation of the good affection of the Fleet and Seamen towards us and the Nation, may be the Prologue to that peace which was first interrupted by the mistake and misunderstanding of their Predecessors, which would be such a blessing unto us all, that We should not be less delighted the manner then the matter of it.

In this hope and confidence, we have sent the inclosed Declaration to you; earnestly desiring you, that you will cause it to be published to all the Officers and Seamen of the Fleet: And you are also to tell them, That we have the same gracious purpose towards them, which we have already expressed to the Army at Land, and will provide to pay for all Arrears. So depending upon Gods blessing, which are best for us all, we bid you farewel.

Given at Our Court at Breda this 14 day of April, 1660. in the 12ᵗʰ year of Our Raign.

At a Council of War held on board the *Naesby* the 3. of *May*, where were present the General, Vice-admiral, Rear-admiral, capt *Cuttance*, cap. *Clark*, cap. *Hayward* cap. *Penrise*, cap *Wager*, cap. *Starling*, and cap. *Mootham* &c. Upon the Generals communicating unto them a letter from his Majesty directed to Gen. *Monck* and himself, bearing date *April* 14. and a Declaration of his Majesty of the same date.

Resolved (*nemine contradicente*)

That the Commanders and Officers of the Fleet do receive the gracious Declaration of his Majesty, as also the expressions of his gracious purposes towards them, and the whole Fleet, (communicated in a Letter to the Generals) with great joyfulness of heart; and for them do return unto his Majesty their most humble thanks, declaring and professing their exact loyalty and duty unto his Majesty, and desire the Generals of the Fleet humbly to represent the same unto him.

It was also Resolved, *That the said Letter, Declaration and Vote, should be publickly read to the respective ships and Companies of the Fleet now in the Downs, to know their sense concerning the same.*

Which being accordingly performed, they did by loud acclamations, and other expressions of Joy, declare their assent to the said *Vote*, not one person in the whole Fleet manifesting any dissent thereunto.

Samuel Pepys, Secretary.

A PROCLAMATION

Although it can no way be doubted, but that his Majesties Right and Title to his Crowns and Kingdoms, is, and was every way Compleated by the Death of his most Royall Father of glorious Memory, without the Ceremony or Solemnity of a Proclamation: Yet since Proclamations in such Cases have been always used, to the end that all good Subjects might upon this occasion testifie their Duty and Respect, And since the Armed violence, and other the Calamities of many years last past, have hitherto deprived Us of any such Opportunity, wherein we might Express Our Loyaltie and Allegiance to his Majesty: We therefore the Lords and Commons now assembled in Parliament, together with the Lord Mayor, Aldermen, and Commons of the City of London, and other Freemen of this Kingdom now present, doe according to Our Duty and Allegeance, heartily, joyfully, and unanimously Acknowledg and Proclaim, That immediately upon the Decease of Our late Soveraign Lord King Charls, the Imperiall Crown of the Realm of England, and of all the Kingdoms, Dominions, and Rights belonging to the same, did by inherent Birthright, and Lawfull and undoubted Succession, Descend and come to His most Excellent Majesty, CHARLS the Second, as being Lineally, Justly, and Lawfully next Heire of the Blood-Royall of this Realm; and that by the Goodness and Providence of Almighty God, He is of *England*, *Scotland*, *France*, and *Ireland*, the most Potent, Mighty, and undoubted King: And thereunto we most humbly and faithfully doe Submit and Oblige Our Selves, Our Heires, and Posterities for Ever.

God save the KING.

Tuesday *May* 8, 1660.

Ordered by the Commons assembled in Parliament, That this Proclamation be forthwith Printed and Published.

WILL: JESSOP Clerk of the Commons House of Parliament.

London, Printed by *Edward Husbands* and *Thomas Newcomb*, Printers to the Commons House of Parliament.

The exiled King's declaration to the Navy and the loyal response which Mountagu and Pepys thoughtfully prepared before the Council of War could discuss it. Pepys signed it, with a shrewd eye to publicity

(*Right*) Charles spent the closing days of his exile at The Hague, conscious – or not – of angelic protectors overhead, proffering the royal emblems

The belated Proclamation of Charles II as king, ordered by Parliament eleven years after his theoretical succession on the death of his father, to regularize the unprecedented events of the Restoration

anchor', and the long-awaited voyage was really begun, the tailors and painters busily at work cutting up yellow cloth to make a crown and royal cipher and in other ways to tone down the republican appearance of the *Naseby*. As they sailed across the North Sea Pepys heard that his old Cambridge tutor Samuel Morland (of whom he held no very high opinion) had just been knighted by Charles for leaking information while working for Cromwell's Secretary of State.

On 14 May Pepys woke to see the Dutch coast, with The Hague clearly in view. *Holland* In no time the inevitable local boatmen were swarming aboard, touting for custom. Eager as Pepys was to explore a foreign country – in his own phrase, 'with child to see any strange thing' – he could not be spared from my Lord's service until after noon.

The sea was choppy. He got well soaked in landing on the beach. But nothing could damp his spirits and, as he took coach for The Hague, he pulled out his flageolet and treated his fellow-passengers to a tune. In so doing he dropped his unfamiliar rapier in the road. He had to give his boy sixpence to run back and find it, its scabbard already damaged by a horse's hoof.

Pepys, with his passion for tidiness, liked The Hague, 'a most neat place in all respects'. The Dutch at this period enjoyed an outstanding reputation for enterprise,

33

efficiency and technical innovation. He was eager to view everything for himself, and, being lucky enough to fall in with a helpful Englishman who knew the town, he kept up his indefatigable sightseeing until ten o'clock at night, by which time the place was lit up by a bright moon. Undeterred by the lateness of the hour, he then went to pay his respects to the nine-year-old Prince of Orange, who had been out when he called earlier. There was no difficulty about obtaining admission. Pepys was a little disappointed by the lack of pomp but thought the Prince 'a very pretty boy'. So, just before meeting the next two Kings of England, whom he was destined to serve all his working life, Pepys unwittingly kissed the hand of their successor, the future William III, whose coming was to terminate his career. Happily spared foreknowledge of this irony, he went off, supped austerely on mutton and salad – The Hague was bursting at the seams with Englishmen – and so to bed, which he shared, in the sociable and matter-of-fact manner of his century, with the Judge Advocate who had come ashore with him. Everything was 'very neat and handsome', though the boy had to make do with sleeping on a bench in the room.

At three o'clock in the morning Pepys was astir again, to see in daylight what he had viewed only under the moon. He acquired another obliging guide, a school-master who spoke good French and English. He admired the Prince's smart bodyguard and the town burghers with their arms and muskets 'as bright as silver'. He no less admired the women, 'many of them very pretty and in good habit, fashionable', and as all the better class of people seemed to speak French or Latin or both, there was no problem of communication. All this put him in mind of Elizabeth, safe in the Buckinghamshire countryside, and he conscientiously bought her a present, a basket. For himself he purchased three books, 'for the love of the binding'. With the Judge Advocate he went to see the great hall used for sessions of the States General. They found it similar to Westminster, 'not so big – but much neater'.

They returned to their ship with some difficulty – getting on and off the sandy beach at Scheveningen was tricky in such rough weather and they saw several boats capsize. My Lord was on board, however, and Pepys had the consolation of supping alone with him and the captain and of observing that Mountagu showed him 'much more respect than ever he did yet'. The bad conditions, sometimes making it impossible for anyone to land or come aboard again, delayed the arrival of the King. After a dull day, when they were reduced to playing ninepins or cards, Pepys managed to get ashore and to The Hague, where he squeezed himself and Mountagu's little son into the King's presence, and kissed the royal hand, as well as the Duke of York's, the future James II. Charles impressed Pepys as 'a very sober man'. His court seemed 'very splendid', but Pepys was under no illusions about his poverty. He had been told, by an eye-witness, of the King's delight when some money had been brought him the previous day – 'so joyful, that he called the Princess Royal and Duke of York to look upon it as it lay in the portmanteau before it was taken out.'

For some days longer the fleet rode the swell off the Dutch coast and Pepys was free to extend his explorations. He went to Delft, 'a most sweet town, with bridges and a river in every street'. Returning by boat along the canal he saw 'a pretty sober Dutch lass' who 'sat reading all the way', and he 'could not fasten any discourse upon her'. On the following evening he ran into an old Cambridge friend who took him to a Dutch house 'where there was an exceeding pretty lass and right for the sport; but it being Saturday, we could not have much of her company'. They sat drinking till midnight, by which time his friend 'was almost drunk'. He saw Pepys to his lodging and then announced that he was going back to 'lie with the girl, which he told me he had done in the morning.'

Pepys himself was held back by timidity rather than virtue. In the early hours of the next morning, finding the sea too rough to get back to the ship, he made up another hour or two's sleep in an inn at Scheveningen, where, as the common practice was, he shared the room with strangers even of the other sex. 'In another bed', the *Diary* records, 'there was a pretty Dutch woman in bed alone; but although I had a month's mind to her, I had not the boldness to go to her.' Later, when she was dressing, he engaged her in conversation as far as he could and, on

A Dutch party playing tric-trac, a form of backgammon

Charles II embarks at
Scheveningen, 23 May 1660

the pretext of admiring her ring, kissed her hand 'but had not the face to offer anything more.'

Eventually he regained the ship with his party, but only after an alarming passage in the boat, when he was soaked to the skin but was the only one to escape being sick. Even so, he was in poor shape, 'partly through last night's drinking and want of sleep', so after a word or two with Mountagu he flung himself down upon his bed and knew no more 'till the 4 a∕clock gun the next morning waked me, which I took for 8 at night that night; and rising to piss, mistook the sun∕rising for the sun∕setting on Sunday night.' After which he relapsed into oblivion for another five hours.

The time for such relaxation was over. A day was spent catching up with the paperwork neglected while he had been ashore. The next morning, 'now beginning to be settled in my wits again', he stood at the captain's elbow to welcome the Duke of York as he came up the gangway. The Duke had been made High Admiral of England a few days before. Dressed 'in yellow trimming', he struck Pepys as a 'very fine' gentleman. It was altogether an exciting day, with much drinking of healths, a harper playing through dinner, and a constant succession of salutes, 'nothing in the world but going of guns almost all this day'. Pepys liked to try everything for himself – on that spree ashore he had met a Dutch bellman in the

street at midnight and insisted on holding his clapper because it reminded him of those used for bird-scaring in the cornfields at home. Now, when the first royal salute was fired in honour of the King, he had to involve himself in the historic moment, and nothing would satisfy him but to discharge the cannon next to his cabin, when he nearly blinded himself in the right eye by holding his head too much over the gun.

The King came aboard the next day, and with such a company of grand personages that the ship's accommodation was strained to the utmost. Pepys had to move to the carpenter's cabin and share even that with a physician, Dr Clerke. His dinners in the captain's state-room were a thing of the past. Now he ate in his cabin, sitting elbow to elbow with Dr Clerke and several others, medical men or royal chaplains. But the atmosphere was so heavy with rejoicing, the King so full of charm and affability, that no one could complain of the temporary discomforts.

One of the King's first acts, in consultation with his brother, was to change those unfortunate ships' names. The *Naseby* became the *Charles*, the *Speaker* became the *Mary*, and so on. Then the anchor was weighed, 'and with a fresh gale and most happy weather we set sail for England – all the afternoon the King walking here and there, up and down (quite contrary to what I thought him to have been), very active and stirring.'

37

The final episode in the King's 1651 escape, recounted to Pepys: a Dutch artist's impression of his dash across the Channel from his hiding-place in Sussex

There, on the quarter-deck, Pepys heard him tell the story of his escape after the battle at Worcester nine years before. Entering up his journal afterwards, he set down a summary of the King's adventures, without any mention of the famous oak-tree episode. Twenty years later, however, when they were at Newmarket together, Charles dictated the whole story to Pepys, who took it down in shorthand.

The second morning found them in sight of Dover, where Monck and a vast assembly of people were waiting to welcome the King. Before landing, the royal brothers pleased everyone by breakfasting democratically on the standard ship's rations of peas, pork and boiled beef. The Duke of York pleased Pepys even more by remembering his name and promising him his future favour.

Altogether, the whole business had gone off in a highly satisfactory manner, and though there was a certain sense of deflation when the royal party had disembarked and begun that triumphal progress to London which he would have dearly loved to share, Pepys had plenty of blessings to count in the quietness of the now half-empty ship. There had been a distribution of royal largesse to the crew and to my Lord's staff: Pepys managed somehow to qualify for a share from both sums, thereby doubling the modest capital he had possessed when he left home.

The shorthand record of the King's escape,
taken down by Pepys at Newmarket in 1680,
when Charles retold him the story

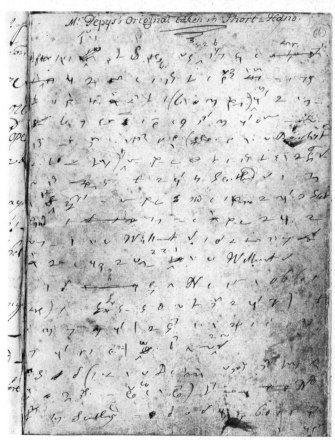

At one stage of his zigzag journey to safety
Charles passed as a servant of
Jane Lane, who rode pillion

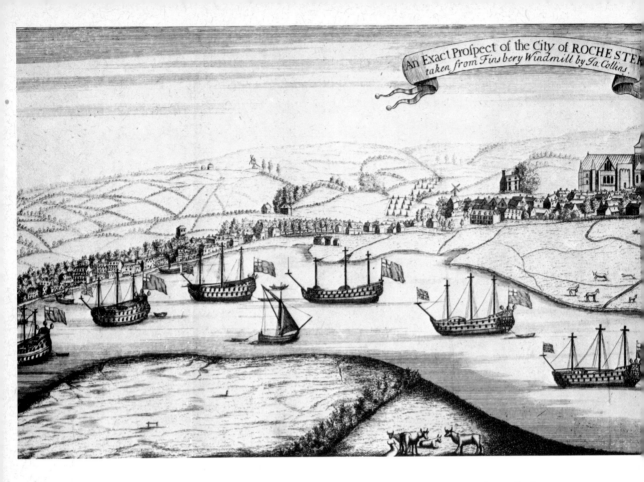

An Exact Prospect of the City of ROCHESTER taken from Finsbery Windmill by Ja. Collins.

He had similarly acquired intangible but invaluable assets through the contacts made while at sea, and he had consolidated his position with Mountagu. His patron was 'almost transported with joy' at the smooth success of the King's return. He had already received the Order of the Garter and was promised the peerage which made him, a few weeks later, Earl of Sandwich, when Monck was made Duke of Albemarle. 'We must have a little patience,' he told Pepys, 'and we will rise together. In the meantime I will do you all the good jobs I can.'

On 7 June my Lord received orders to proceed to London, and early next morning Pepys disembarked with him, took horse at Deal, and reached Canterbury in time for dinner. Pepys characteristically did not miss the chance to slip into the cathedral and see Becket's tomb. Then they were off again, through Rochester, where he noted the famous stone bridge with its eleven arches, to Gravesend, where he supped with my Lord, drank late with a certain Captain Penrose, and retired to bed 'weary and hot', after kissing 'a good handsome wench . . . the first that I have seen a great while.' Relief for the returning voyager was at hand. Two nights later his *Diary* was able to record, 'To bed with my wife.'

'We will rise together,' Mountagu promised
Pepys after the King's smooth return. He had
just received the Garter and was about to
become Earl of Sandwich. (*Left*) Rochester: the
famous stone bridge with its eleven arches was
dominated by the equally famous castle.
(*Below*) Canterbury Cathedral: though riding
hard to reach London, Pepys characteristically
found time during the halt for dinner to visit
Becket's tomb

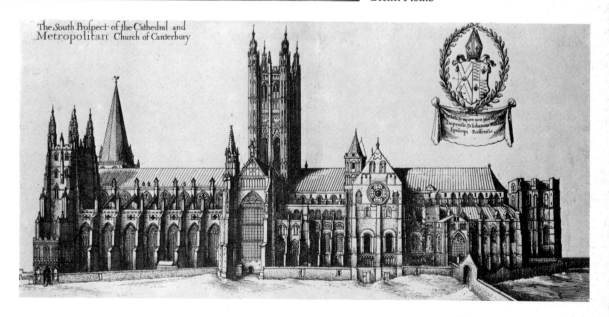

The South Prospect of the Cathedral and
Metropolitan Church of Canterbury

My Lord was as good as his word. During the Commonwealth the civil administration of the Navy had been run by a committee. Now, under the Duke of York as High Admiral, it was proposed to reconstitute the old Navy Board with six senior officials having various responsibilities, and a 'Clerk of the Acts'. He obtained a promise of this post for Pepys. It carried a salary of £350, which could be vastly increased with all the perquisites and presents then regarded as legitimate for the holder of a public office to accept. It carried status, too, and residential accommodation next door to the department, situated in Seething Lane, a stone's throw from Tower Hill.

Pepys grew more and more excited as he realized all the advantages of such an appointment, but the next week or two's entries in the *Diary* reflect a mounting anxiety, and remind us that 'the rat race' is merely a new phrase, not a new development. Within a few days he received a proposition that he should accept £500 to stay out of the running. Then, to his dismay, he learnt that Thomas Barlow, who had held the clerkship before its abolition under the Commonwealth, was still alive and might claim that he was still the holder. My Lord advised Pepys to get possession of his patent, and promised to do all he could to keep Barlow out. Getting the patent, even after he had obtained his warrant from the Duke of York, was no formality but a bureaucratic obstacle course which gave him several days of breathless apprehension.

He had to get his warrant from the Attorney General's office ('which cost me seven pieces') and take it to the Privy Seal. Then his patent must be engrossed in proper form, so he hastened to the House of Lords for advice from an old friend, Kipps, now Seal Bearer to the Lord Chancellor. Kipps referred him to a Chancery clerk named Beale, who would do the job for him, but Beale proved obstructive and said he had no time. The Restoration had produced a rush of business. Never had there been so many people frantic to have their new honours and appointments safely confirmed in black and white. Pepys 'was forced to run all up and down Chancery Lane and the Six Clerks' Office, but could find none that could write that hand that were at leisure', the 'hand' being the Chancery script required in such documents. Pepys was now almost beside himself, for he had just heard of old Barlow's presence in town and his intention to claim his former post. At 11 o'clock at night Pepys got hold of an obliging Chancery clerk named Spong, who promised to write out the patent by the next morning, when Pepys called on him and found him, true to his undertaking, busy at his task in his dressing gown.

The end was in sight, but still uncertain. Pepys hastened to the Chancellor's for a receipt and thence to the unhelpful Beale for a 'docket' identifying the patent as what it was. Beale was even more unpleasant than before, refusing on the grounds that 'it was ill writ (because I had got it writ by another hand and not by him)', but by giving him two pieces, 'after which it was strange how civil and tractable he

James, Duke of York, as High Admiral, dressed not for sea-going but in the conventional trappings of classical antiquity

was', Pepys obtained the docket. He then had to break off and attend a long meeting at the Navy Office – where at least he was already discharging his duties, though still on tenterhooks about his future security. Then it was back to Beale once more, who had everything ready for sealing and arranged to meet him at the Chancellor's office in an hour's time. There, thanks to his friend Kipps and some persistent use of Mountagu's name, 'I did beyond all expectation get my seal passed.' Even so, while it was being done in another room, he was embarrassed to encounter Sir George Carteret, the head of the Navy Office. Pepys did not want to confess what he was doing there and had to hold his chief in conversation while the last stage was safely completed. After which, he rushed home, collected Elizabeth, and swept her off in triumph to Seething Lane to see their future home at the Navy Office, and she, like him, was 'mightily pleased at all things there'.

43

Sept.

the interest of this Kingdom to have a peace with Spaine, and a war with France and Holland. Whereon Sir R. Ford talked like a man of great reason and experience. And afterward did send for a Cupp of Tee (a China drink) of which I never had drank before) and went away. Then come Sir Birch and his R. Browne (by a former appointment; and with them from Towre Wharfe in the barge belonging to our Office, we went to Deptford, to pay off the Ship Success. Which, (Sir G. Carteret and Sir W. Penn afterward coming to us) we did, (Col Rich being a mighty busy man, and one that is the most indefatigable and forward to make himself work, of any man that ever I knew in my life. At the Globe we had a very good dinner, and after that to the pay again, which being finished, we returned by water again. And I, from our Office with Col Slingsby by coach to Westminster, (I setting him down at his lodgings by the way)

A typical passage from the Diary, as transcribed by Joseph Smith in 1819–22. It records Pepys's first cup of tea, consumed 25 September 1660. (*Right*) Sir William Penn, an experienced Commonwealth admiral, Pepys's colleague on the Board and his neighbour.

Seething Lane

They moved into the house a few days later, though what with redecorations and improvements – such as the making of a door he had set his heart on, to give access from his room to the flat roof – it was Christmas before the *Diary* could record the house 'once more clear of workmen . . . and clean'. Such discomforts he could tolerate. Indeed, it suited him to keep everything under his eye, fussing over the workmen and seeing that he was not cheated. What really mattered was to be entrenched in his new position. He threw himself into his duties with enthusiasm.

Navy Board

It would have been understandable if he had contented himself with a prudently subordinate stance towards his colleagues. They were middle-aged, influential men, nearly all with long experience of naval matters. Sir George Carteret, now Treasurer, had been Comptroller as far back as 1639. Sir William Batten, the Surveyor, had first held that post in 1638. Sir William Penn had distinguished himself as a Commonwealth admiral. Peter Pett, the resident Commissioner at Chatham dockyard, came of the family that had built all the principal English warships for the past century. The other members of the Board, Lord Berkeley of Stratton and the Comptroller, Colonel Slingsby, were men of considerable

Peter Pett, eminent shipbuilder, a naval commissioner mainly occupied at the Chatham yards

authority. In such company Pepys, twenty-seven, with no more than a few weeks' purely clerical experience aboard ship, might easily have been pushed into the role of office boy.

He was not. His love of method, his grasp of detail, his capacity for working long hours, his inquiring mind that drove him always to find out for himself – these qualities, together with an ambitious trait which offset any undue deference to his superiors, enabled him to hold his own with his eminent associates, of whom he became in due time increasingly critical.

Fortunately, they were easy-going men. Only Penn and Batten had living quarters adjoining the Office, and they gave an affable welcome to their young colleague and his pretty wife. Slingsby was no less friendly and drew on his long experience – his father had been Comptroller before him – to inform Pepys on the history of the department. His death, little more than a year later, was a sad loss. Lord Berkeley and Sir George Carteret were grand figures who did little but appear at the twice-weekly Board meetings. And Pett was down at Chatham, occupied with the dockyards. So it was not difficult for Pepys, by degrees, to draw more and more of the departmental strings into his own hands.

It helped, too, that England was at peace. The paying-off of ships and the disposal of surplus stores were the main business. Finance, of course, was a worry. 'To Whitehall,' Pepys noted on 31 July, 'where my Lord and the Principal Officers met and had great discourse about raising of money for the Navy; which is in very sad condition, and money must be raised for it.' Money could only come from Parliament. Five days later he had to appear before 'a Committee of Parliament . . . to give them an answer to an order of theirs, that we could not give them any account of the accounts of the Navy in the year 36, 37, 38, 39, 40 – as they desire.'

Whitehall Palace, the real seat of power. A miniature town rather than a building, it occupied 23 acres

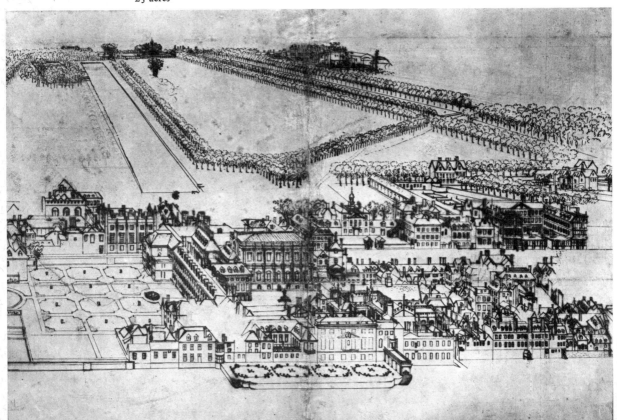

Edward Hyde, Lord Clarendon: Charles's adviser in exile and until 1667, when he was made the scapegoat for the naval disaster. His daughter was the Duke of York's first wife and bore the future Queens Mary II and Anne. *(Right)* Ashley Cooper, 1st Earl of Shaftesbury, founder of the Whig party and bitterly opposed to the Duke of York, whom he tried to exclude from the succession

Pepys did not live like a modern civil servant, however, with the ever-present shadow of Parliamentary questions. There were occasions, but they were comparatively rare, when the Navy Board had to justify itself at Westminster. On 25 November 1664 the *Diary* begins: 'Up and at my office all the morning, to prepare an account of the charge we have been put to extraordinary by the Dutch already; and I have brought it to appear £852,700; but God knows this is only a scare to the Parliament, to make them give the more money.' He was rewarded by hearing, later the same day, that the House had voted the King two and a half million pounds 'only for the Navy'. When things went badly wrong, as in the humiliating Medway disaster of 1667, Parliament again could not be ignored.

The seventeenth-century House was not, of course, in full-time session as it is today, for there was not the constant stream of legislation and other business to occupy it. The Convention which had restored the King was replaced in the following year by the 'Cavalier' Parliament, which survived, with replacements at by-elections, until January 1679. It was followed, in that and the next two years, by three short-lived Parliaments each with an overwhelming Whig majority, which the King kept dissolving because they tried to pass the Exclusion Bill preventing his Catholic brother's succession to the throne. For the last four years of his reign Parliament did not meet at all.

For Pepys, therefore, the seat of power was not in the ordinary way Westminster but Whitehall, Restoration Whitehall, that is, a royal palace where regularly he had to seek out, amid the throngs of courtiers, sightseers, petitioners, courtesans and others, either the King himself or the High Admiral, James, or my Lord or whatever other great personage was needed to signify approval or exert influence. Whitehall was open to the world. Anyone who had once been granted the entrée was entitled thereafter to walk in and parade the Stone Gallery or watch the King at dinner. Whitehall was the place to learn what was happening, to get things done, to circumvent one's rivals. 'It runs through the galleries' was the contemporary phrase equivalent to our 'well-informed sources' and 'lobby gossip'. The government was the King and his immediate advisers – Charles thought even a thirty-strong Privy Council inconveniently large. In his later years he was able to dispense with Parliament by living on independent sources of income, such as customs revenue and subsidies from his cousin, Louis XIV.

This, then, was the world of Pepys's working life: home and office adjoining in Seething Lane, visits to Whitehall Palace, where the Duke had fine apartments overlooking the river, rarer appearances at Westminster, and occasional journeys further afield to naval establishments at Chatham, Deptford, Woolwich, or even Portsmouth.

In his first months he went through the files, made an inventory of the Board's papers, mastered the procedure, and familiarized himself with the limits of his own authority. He was learning all the time, and from everyone. He got a clerk to instruct him in the jargon of sailors, and a lieutenant from the former *Naseby* to go over a ship's model, explaining every part of the vessel and its function. On a

Portsmouth, then as now a naval establishment, necessitating an occasional visit from Pepys

Henry Bennet, later Earl of Arlington: Ashley Cooper's colleague in the famous 'Cabal' ministry which displaced Lord Clarendon in 1667. (*Right*) George Villiers, Duke of Buckingham: one of the five 'Cabal' ministers, Charles's favourite and the Duke of York's enemy, and so hostile to Pepys

Officers	Deptford	Woolwich	Chatham	Portsmo:
Clerke of the Checque	80.0.0	70.0.0	120.0.0	68.13.10
His Instruments & pap mony	1 18.5.0	1 18.5.0	2 61.0.0	19.5.0
Storekeeper	144.18.4	70.0.0	1 100.0.0	50.0.0
His Clerkes & paper money	1 19.5.0	1 18.5.0	1 24.5.0	19.5.0
Storekeepers assistant	2 57.7.8		2 57.7.8	
Ma.r ettendants	1 100.0.0		2 200.0.0	1 100.0.0
Assistants ma.r ettend.ts		20.0.0		
Clerke of the Survey	60.0.0		100.0.0	52.0.0
Ma.r Shipwright	114.10.0		104.10.0	132.6.8
Shipwr.t Assistant	1 70.0.0	1 70.0.0	1 70.0.0	57.0.10
Chirurgeon	30.8.4	30.8.4	13.6.8	
Ma.r Calker			70.0.0	47.0.8
Boatswaine of y.e yard	35.0.0	60.0.0	60.0.0	40.0.0
Porter of the yard	17.14.8	16.6.8	13.6.8	17.10.0
Plugkeeper		6.1.8	6.0.0	
Locke-out			38.0.0	
Keeper of y.e Payhouse			14.0.0	
Clerke of y.e Ropeyard		60.0.0	70.0.0	40.0.0
Ma.r Ropemaker		50.0.0	44.0.0	44.0.0
Porter of y.e Ropehouse	12.3.4		13.6.8	
Purveyor of Timber	60.0.0	60.0.0		
Messenger to y.e Treas.r	18.5.0			

A typical page from the Pocket Book, prepared by Pepys for the guidance of his master, the Duke of York

Pepys's conscientious attention to detail is shown in his 'Navy White Book', which he kept partly in shorthand

March. 26. 1664.

A tryall of y difference of measure & weight between Stockh. & Russia Tarr.

Deptford: a naval base where a visit from Pepys was an important occasion, 'all the captains of the fleet coming cap in hand to us'

typical visit to Deptford he 'viewed old pay-books, and found that the Commanders did never heretofore receive any pay for the rigging time, but only for sea-time, contrary to what . . . Sir W. Batten told the Duke the other day. I also searched all the ships in the Wet Dock for fire, and found all in good order, it being very dangerous for the King that so many of his ships lie together there. I was among the canvas in stores also, with Mr Harris, the sailmaker, and learnt the difference between one sort and another, to my great content. . . .'

For all his nosiness not even Pepys could grasp everything, as he was ready to admit in the privacy of his journal. Thus, on a visit to my Lord, he stayed to attend a committee meeting 'to sit upon the contract for the Mole, which I dare say none of us that were there understood, but yet they agreed of things as Mr Cholmely and Sir J. Lawson demanded . . . and so I left them to go on to agree, for I understood it not.' He had learnt at least the trick of sitting poker-faced in committee, allowing silence to be mistaken for deliberation.

As he had demonstrated during those days aboard the *Naseby*, he was prepared to work early and late to ensure that everything was in order and the letters answered punctually. It was the same at Seething Lane. 'So to my office all the afternoon,' records the *Diary* on a Sunday in January, 1663, 'writing orders myself to have ready against tomorrow, that I might not appear negligent to Mr Coventry' – Coventry being the Duke of York's secretary, and later a staunch supporter of Pepys. That same Sunday evening he went next door to Sir William Penn's, where Batten and other members of the Board dropped in and they 'talked about

The *Britannia*, finest of all the new ships Pepys added to the Navy. Going with Hewer to inspect her at Gillingham, he was entertained on board with a bowl of punch

business'. When they broke up, Pepys accompanied Batten to his house and they had more talk, and drank cider. After all that, he still returned to his office and put in another short spell at his desk.

'Up betimes and to my office' is the recurrent refrain of the weekday entries, 4 o'clock the commonly mentioned hour, or 5 o'clock in winter. Exceptions are conscientiously noted. Sometimes he 'lay late', either in lengthy argument with Elizabeth or affectionately relaxed. At other times he admitted to having been fuddled the night before. On occasions he kept his room 'having taken physic'. He and his contemporaries, including my Lord, seem continually to have been taking physic, and of so drastic a nature that they dared not venture forth.

Social life For all his zeal, Pepys was certainly not absorbed in his duties to the exclusion of all else. 'Early and late' was often a literal description of his office day, the interval being crammed with multifarious interests and activities. After that initial onslaught on his departmental papers he would go for his 'morning draught', frequently at some convenient tavern. This was in fact his breakfast, but might have a social character more akin to that of a modern lunch. By chance meeting or

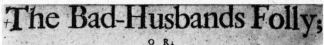

A convivial scene in a tavern, which the Clerk of the Acts would have enjoyed as much as anyone. (*Right*) Gossip in a tavern: a woodcut from Pepys's collection of ballads

by arrangement he might take it with ships' captains or City merchants, old schoolfellows or his former Exchequer colleagues, or his father when there were family problems to be sorted out. The refreshment might run to a peck of oysters and a glass of mulled white wine, anchovies, mince pie and a collar of brawn, or simply 'cakes and ale'.

Dinner, taken from midday onwards, was no less sociable. In a typical month, November 1662, he dined out eleven times. At home, there were frequently guests. Arrangements were extremely flexible: in the heart of London food and drink were always available. Once Pepys took a friend home rather late and found that Elizabeth had already dined, so the two men went round the corner to a tavern and ordered a couple of lobsters. Elizabeth was not invariably in – she might be shopping or visiting, and Pepys often dined alone without allowing any hint of indignation to creep into his journal. Wherever he found himself during the day, either on business or on pleasure, there was seldom any problem about meals, either at a friend's or at a tavern. One day it could be a formal dinner at Trinity House, of which he became a junior member in 1661 and Master fifteen years later. On another he might eat with his departmental colleagues at one of their favourite resorts, the Dolphin, close by. He not infrequently dined with my Lord at his official residence, the Wardrobe, near St Paul's, or, if my Lord was absent at sea, then with my Lady. Lady Sandwich was as warmly disposed to Pepys as was her husband, and the friendliness was extended to Elizabeth, who went there too, either with Samuel or by herself. Only when the Earl and Countess were entertaining very grand guests did the Pepyses revert, uncomplainingly, to their status of poor relations, and take their dinner in another room.

'Poor' was by this time only a relative term. From the moment he became securely established at the Navy Office Pepys never looked back. He could pay his 'club', or share, in any ordinary company, and keep up the appearance proper to his status, though he never quite lost the frugal habits inbred in early years. It sometimes hurt to spend the money, and the *Diary* records many a twinge of pain at the end of the day, but his love of life (including his love for the sometimes irritating girl he had married) almost always triumphed over his instinct for economy. In his first few weeks at the office he had been tempted to sell his new post for cash – he was offered a thousand pounds ('which made my mouth water') but although the buying and selling of such positions was accepted practice, he had turned down the offer on my Lord's advice. As his cousin reminded him, 'it was not the salary of any place that did make a man rich, but the opportunities of getting money while he is in the place.'

Those opportunities were many and various. Within reason, like the purchase of commissions and appointments, they were universally recognized in England, and abroad, as a legitimate supplement to the inadequate remuneration a public servant received from his government. Pepys accepted many gifts, small and not so small, in cash and kind – 'five pieces of gold' from Mr Throgmorton, a merchant, 'for to do him a small piece of service about a convoy to Bilbao', or four dozen bottles of wine from a captain just returned from Spain. The *Diary* is full of such entries. 'Two letters from some that I had done a favour to, which brought me in each a piece of gold. . . .' Five pounds from a captain for whom Pepys had obtained the command of a ship. . . . But such *douceurs* could not sway him against his conscience and he was more scrupulous than some of his colleagues. In June 1663, with the self-confidence born of three years' experience, he 'had a difference with Sir W. Batten about Mr Bowyer's tar, which I am resolved to cross, though he sent me last night, as a bribe, a barrel of sturgeon, which, it may be, I shall send back, for I will not have the King abused so abominably in the price of what we buy, by Sir W. Batten's corruption and underhand dealing.'

There were moments when Pepys, like Clive a century later, stood astonished at his own moderation. A few months after the dispute over the tar, he 'sat all the morning making a great contract with Sir W. Warren for £3,000 worth of masts,'

Coffee houses first appeared
in London in 1656 and
became popular resorts
in the Restoration period

and noted in his journal, 'but, good God! to see what a man might do, were I a knave, the whole business from beginning to end being done by me out of the office, and signed to by them upon the once reading of it to them, without the least care or consultation either of quality, price, number, or need of them, only in general that it was good to have a store. But I hope my pains was such, as the King has the best bargain of masts has been bought these 27 years in this office.'

Whatever temptations he resisted, Pepys now enjoyed a good standard of living and a steady increase in his capital, noted at regular intervals with undisguised satisfaction. The modest establishment at Axe Yard had grown by the end of 1660: the single servant, Jane, had a boy to help her, her brother Wayneman, while a seventeen-year-old youth, William Hewer, was employed part-time as Pepys's clerk in the office and part-time as a general factotum in the house. Within a few years there were four maids. And, though Pepys continually lamented the expense, money never seems to have been lacking for new furnishings, clothes, books and fine bookcases, and the provision of hospitality suited to his place in society.

William Hewer

There was money, too, to commission portraits of himself and Elizabeth, and to engage teachers of singing and dancing for them both. Sittings, lessons and music practice were just a few of the occupations fitted into those full days, along with the office work, the sociable 'morning draughts', and the no less sociable dinners and suppers that followed. There were visits to coffee-houses and the

55

Lincoln's Inn Fields, with train bands drilling.

newly reopened theatres, where sometimes he had the grace to be embarrassed at being recognized in working hours. He could never withstand the lure of an unusual spectacle, be it an execution, or a wrestling match between Cornishmen and Cumbrians, or the ceremonious arrival of the Russian ambassador on 27 November 1662.

On that morning, fittingly, he woke to 'find the tops of the houses covered with snow, which is a rare sight, that I have not seen these three years'. After a few hours at the office he and his colleagues went out to see the City train bands paraded on Tower Hill, with the Life Guards and 'most of the wealthy citizens in their black velvet coats and gold chains'. After a long delay the Russians arrived. He could not see the ambassador inside his coach but he was impressed by the attendants in their fur caps, 'very handsome comely men, and most of them with hawks upon their fists to present to the King. But Lord,' he concludes, with one of those typical comments which bring him close to the modern reader, 'to see the absurd nature of Englishmen, that cannot forbear laughing and jeering at everything that looks strange.'

There was not a fur-capped Muscovite mission to enliven every day, but Pepys seldom if ever knew boredom. At bedtime he was content to record a quiet stroll under the trees in the Temple, or in the new garden at Lincoln's Inn, or in St James's Park, where the King might sometimes be glimpsed with a flurry of little spaniels round his feet, walking with nervous speed to avoid being buttonholed by petitioners. Nor, though he delighted in company, did he fear solitude. 'At noon

But the new garden afforded a quieter place in which to stroll

played on my theorbo,' he notes happily. At other times he might be studying
mathematics or geography, reading Fuller's *Worthies* or the text of an old play, or
just handling the fine bindings of his beloved books and contemplating the best
way to arrange them. And there was always the secret pleasure of writing up his
journal and turning back its pages to savour the essence of former days.

Such was the life on which Pepys entered from the moment his appointment was
sealed and he took up his abode in Seething Lane, but the relaxed self-confidence
came only by degrees, and to begin with he was at full stretch, meeting the demands
of his new situation. 'Never since I was a man in the world,' he confessed as he
wrote up his journal for 10 August 1660, 'was I ever so great a stranger to public
affairs as now I am, having not read a newsbook or anything like it, or enquired
after any news, or what the Parliament doth or in any wise how things go.'

In fact, while he was getting used to his position as Clerk of the Acts, Charles II *Restoration*
was accustoming himself to being King – and England to having one again, and
to the end of all the Puritan restrictions that for years had imposed a superficial and
unpopular austerity on the nation.

The Restoration brought no wholesale blood-bath or campaign of victimization.
Just as my Lord had fought under Cromwell at Naseby, so men like Carteret and
Penn had served on opposite sides in the Civil War but could now work amicably
together at the Navy Office. Only those held personally responsible for the execu-
tion of Charles I were made to pay the grim price in full. 'I went out to Charing
Cross,' wrote Pepys on 13 October, 'to see Major-General Harrison hanged,

drawn, and quartered . . . he looking as cheerfully as any man could do in that condition. . . . Thus it was my chance to see the King beheaded at Whitehall and to see the first blood shed in revenge for the blood of the King at Charing Cross.' He then enjoyed some oysters with two friends at the Sun tavern and went home, 'where I was angry with my wife for her things lying about, and in my passion kicked the little fine basket which I bought her in Holland and broke it, which troubled me. . . .' After the violence of the morning he soothed his ruffled temper indoors all the afternoon, 'setting up shelves in my study'. Though, like most of his contemporaries, he seemed unable to stay away from the barbaric spectacle of an execution, he thought it 'a sad sight' to see the remains of the regicides impaled in public view, and when the bodies of Cromwell, Ireton and others were exhumed and hung from the gallows he was troubled 'that a man of so great courage as [Cromwell] should have that dishonour, though otherwise he might deserve it enough.'

Coronation   A happier kind of spectacle was afforded by the Coronation in the following April. On the preceding day, having 'made myself as fine as I could' in a new velvet coat he had been keeping for the occasion, Pepys watched the King and his brother pass in procession from the Tower to Whitehall. Next morning he got into Westminster Abbey soon after four o'clock, 'with much ado' for on this day the Clerk to the Acts had no privileges. He squeezed himself into a stand in the north transept and at eleven the King arrived, his sceptre carried by my Lord. To his chagrin Pepys could not see the solemnities enacted in the choir and the music was lost because of the general hubbub. He was compensated afterwards by being able to witness all the traditional pomp of the banquet in Westminster Hall, with the King's Champion 'all in armour on horseback' and the King's new French-style string orchestra of twenty-four violins.

'A sad sight': the Royalist revenge on the surviving regicides and the exhumation of those, such as Cromwell, already dead

Part of the coronation procession of Charles II in April 1661 ▶

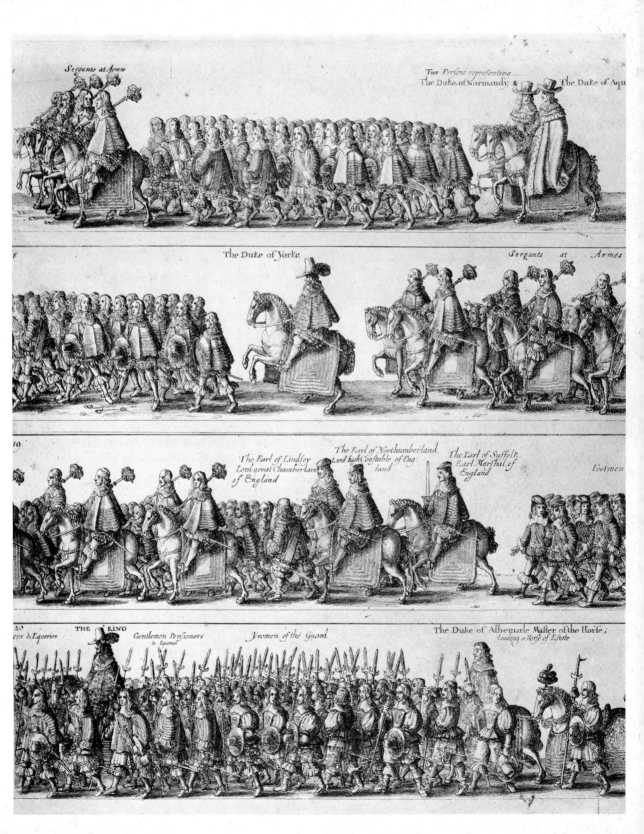

Sergants at Armes

Two Persons representing
The Duke of Normandy, & The Duke of Aqu

The Duke of Yorke

Sergants at Armes

19

The Earl of Lindsey
Lord great Chamberlain
of England

The Earl of Northumberland
Lord high Constable of Eng:
land

The Earl of Suffolk
Earl Marshal of
England

Footmen

20

ers & Equeries

THE KING

Gentlemen Pensioners
& Equeries

Yeomen of the Guard

The Duke of Albemarle Master of the Horse;
leading a Horse of Estate

The King enjoys his own again:
Charles II in his coronation robes.

As night fell, the fun outside grew faster and more furious. 'The City,' he wrote next day with splitting head, 'had a light like a glory round it, with bonfires.' He 'wondered to see how the ladies did tipple'. Not Elizabeth – so far as he knew – for he had placed her with other friends, to leave himself free. He staggered to his own bed in poor shape. 'If ever I was foxed it was now.'

The following evening, as he brought his journal up to date, he declared that after 'the sight of these glorious things, I may now shut my eyes against any other objects, or for the future trouble myself to see things of state and show, as being sure never to see the like again in this world.' But his old buoyancy was returning. He had written only a few more lines when he heard the splendid noise of the fireworks going off along the river. 'And I wish myself with them,' he admitted, 'being sorry not to see them. So to bed.'

The festivities had seen the crowning not only of the King but of the whole process of restoring – so far as it was possible to put back the clock – the way of life England had known before the Civil War. The long-forbidden maypoles had

60

gone up even before Parliament had voted for the King's return. By the time Pepys followed him back to London there were obvious signs of change. On his second Sunday at home he noted that the organs, which the Puritans had removed from the churches, 'did begin to play at Whitehall before the King', though he did not himself hear them until 8 July, when, he wrote, 'I heard very good music, the first time that I remember ever to have heard the organs and singing-men in surplices in my life. The Bishop of Chichester preached before the King and made a great flattering sermon, which I did not like that clergy should meddle with matters of state.' On the whole Pepys, with his passion for music, rejoiced at its reappearance in the churches – a few Sundays later he enjoyed 'a brave anthem', the solo parts of which were sung by Captain Henry Cooke, Master of the Children of the Chapel Royal – but the ritual did not please him, seeming overdone, and he was critical of sermons. The *Diary* that summer includes such admissions as 'spent my time walking up and down in Westminster Abbey all sermon time', chatting with two friends, and again 'spent (God forgive me) most of my time in looking upon Mrs Butler.' Fair women and fine music were what chiefly uplifted him in church, and in both respects the Restoration brightened his Sabbath considerably.

The actors were as swift as the Anglicans to establish themselves again and soon Pepys was able to recapture the childhood delight he had once known at the Red Bull in Clerkenwell. There had been no plays in London for eighteen years, though towards the end of Cromwell's life Sir William Davenant had briefly circumvented the ban by presenting his *Siege of Rhodes* as an 'opera'. But by 1660 Davenant was prudently abroad with the royal exiles, as was another pre-war dramatist, Thomas Killigrew, whom Pepys noted as 'a merry droll, but a gentleman of great esteem', walking the deck as they sailed back with Charles from Holland.

It was these two men, Davenant and Killigrew, who were chiefly responsible for re-opening the theatres, but the ground was ready. Before the King could issue the patents giving them the monopoly to manage the only two permitted play-houses – and while, indeed, Pepys was still clearing up his cabin before disem-barkation – the Red Bull was presenting Ben Jonson's *Epicœne* and the Duke of York had been to see it. By 18 August Pepys had seen his first play at the Cockpit Theatre in Drury Lane, Fletcher's tragicomedy *The Loyal Subject* (a shrewdly chosen box-office title), in which a twenty-year-old youth, Edward Kynaston, played the Duke's sister, Olympia, 'but made the loveliest lady that ever I saw in my life – only, her voice not very good.' After the performance Pepys and his friends entertained young Kynaston and another member of the cast with drinks.

By the end of the year actresses were taking over the female parts. Pepys went to Killigrew's Theatre Royal in Vere Street on 3 January 1661 to see Fletcher and Massinger's comedy, *The Beggars' Bush*, which he had already seen in November with an all-male cast. Now, however, it was 'the first time that ever I saw women

Sir William Davenant, theatre-manager and dramatist, with Killigrew chiefly responsible for reopening the playhouses. He was Shakespeare's godson and, by unsubstantiated tradition, rather more. (*Left below*) A scene from the *Empress of Morocco* at the Dorset Garden Theatre: this playhouse was built by Wren to Davenant's requirements, and Betterton lived on the premises. (*Right below*) A performance in progress, most probably at the Red Bull, Clerkenwell, where Pepys gained his first taste for the theatre as a child

Thomas Betterton, the outstanding actor of the day, admired equally as Hamlet and as Sir Toby Belch. (*Right above*) John Dryden had his first play produced in 1663, and later wrote *Secret Love* with a plot suggested by the King and an excellent part for Nell Gwynn. (*Right*) Thomas Killigrew, founder of Drury Lane Theatre: his own play, *The Parson's Wedding*, made even Pepys blush

come upon the stage.' Not surprisingly Pepys liked the innovation. The very next day he went to Beaumont and Fletcher's *The Scornful Lady*, still with a boy in the title-role, but when he saw it (for the third time) some weeks later it was 'now done by a woman, which makes the play appear much better than ever it did to me.'

At the playhouse he entered yet another world, colourful, poetic and romantic – for 'Restoration drama' was not born overnight, and most of the pieces were at first revivals or adaptations of Elizabethan and Jacobean plays. There was a fair amount of Shakespeare and Pepys was soon recording a visit to *The Moor of Venice* and the distress of 'a very pretty lady that sat by me' when Desdemona was smothered. In the main, however, the public taste favoured playwrights like Beaumont and Fletcher, who, Dryden said in his *Essay of Dramatic Poesy*, 'understood and imitated the conversation of gentlemen much better.' This was important, for the revived theatre was dominated by the Court and a sophisticated minority. Dryden himself, a contemporary of Pepys at Cambridge but not a friend, made his own debut as a playwright with *The Wild Gallant* in 1663.

Pepys followed the fashion in viewing Shakespeare with a critical eye. He began respectfully enough, buying the text of *Henry IV* as he passed St Paul's Churchyard on his way to the performance, 'but my expectation being too great, it did not please me as otherwise I believe it would; and my having a book I believe did spoil it a little.' He was happier after *Hamlet*, 'done with scenes very well . . . Betterton did the Prince's part beyond imagination.' He unfortunately attended the opening performance of *Romeo and Juliet*, when none of the company was word-perfect, and he resolved not to make that mistake again. He thought the play itself 'the worst that ever I heard in my life', but even worse awaited him six months later when he sat through *Midsummer Night's Dream*, 'which I have never seen before, nor shall ever again, for it is the most insipid ridiculous play that ever I saw in my life. I saw, I confess, some good dancing and some handsome women, which was all my pleasure.'

His contribution to the history of the Restoration theatre was not as a critic, though he enjoyed discussion and records arbitrating between friends in a tavern, 'over the best venison pasty that ever I eat of in my life', when they debated whether 'it was essential to a tragedy to have the argument of it true'. But first and foremost, despite his grumbling, he was an enthusiast, an addict who could not keep away, though the guilty consciousness of time and money spent drove him to solemn vows of abstention, kept for as long as six months. In April and May, 1668, on the other hand, he went to the theatre thirty times. There were only the two licensed playhouses, but their repertory changed continually. In any case he was quite happy to see the same piece again.

Written for his own eye alone, and not to instruct posterity, the *Diary* has no systematic account of those other innovations, apart from the actresses, which were

This composite portrait shows John Lacy, one of the King's favourite actors, in three of his most admired roles, Teague in *The Committee*, Scruple in *The Cheats* and Galliard in *The Variety*

making the Restoration theatre so different from its predecessor – the oblong audi-torium derived from the tennis court, the proscenium arch, the scenery and the artificial lighting. The *Diary*'s charm and value lie in the incidental glimpses, as when Pepys went back-stage at the King's Theatre during the 'altering of the stage to make it wider.' 'God knows', he comments wistfully, 'when they will begin to act again; but my business here was to see the inside of the stage and all the tiring-rooms and machines; and indeed it was a sight worthy seeing. But to see their clothes, and the various sorts, and what a mixture of things there was; here a wooden leg, there a ruff, here a hobby-horse, there a crown, would make a man split himself to see with laughing; and particularly Lacy's wardrobe. . . . But then again to think how fine they show on the stage by candle-light, and how poor things they are to look at too near hand. . . .'

At William Berkeley's tragicomedy, *The Lost Lady*, he 'was troubled to be seen by four of our office clerks, which sat in the half-crown box and I in the 1s. 6d.' On another occasion, only two days after renewing his vows to abstain from theatre-going for another three months, he had the chance to slip into a performance of James Shirley's tragedy, *The Cardinal*, in the King's private theatre at Whitehall,

Catherine of Braganza, Charles's long-suffering Portuguese bride: my Lord Sandwich escorted her from Lisbon in 1662, and she inspired Pepys to erotic day-dreams. (*Right*) Nell Gwynn, whose looks and comic spirit charmed Pepys, though, as the King's mistress, she was beyond his reach

which presumably did not count as a breach of his oath, since it was an evening affair, not cutting into his office work, and involving no admission charge. Follow-ing some other gentlemen he 'crept through a narrow place and came into one of the boxes next the King's'. He could not, to his regret, see either the King or his new Queen, Catherine of Braganza, whom my Lord had recently escorted to England from Portugal, but he gained a close view of many other 'fine ladies, who yet are not really so handsome as I used to take them to be'. His own neighbours proved all to be Frenchmen, 'but, Lord! what sport they made to ask a pretty lady that they got among them, that understood both French and English, to make her tell them what the actors said.'

Had Pepys been truly a courtier, and not a civil servant visiting Whitehall primarily on business, his circle of friends might have included men like Davenant and Killigrew. As it was, he had no close contacts with the managers and play-wrights, though he had his back-stage associations with some of the players, notably Henry Harris, 'a very curious and understanding person in all pictures and other things, and a man of fine conversation', and the lively Mrs Knipp, whose dressing-room he visited and with whom he conducted one of his faint-hearted, fumbling love affairs.

Nell Gwynn he admired from afar – royal favour made her forbidden territory – but meeting her informally back-stage on his way to see Mrs Knipp, he came on her 'dressing herself' and 'all unready', and found her even 'prettier than I thought'. When she played in Dryden's new play, *Secret Love, or The Maiden Queen*, the plot of which the King had suggested to the author, Pepys wrote enthusiastically: 'the truth is, there is a comical part done by Nell, which is Florimel, that I never can hope ever to see the like done again, by man or woman . . . both as a mad girl, then most and best of all when she comes in like a young gallant; and hath the motions and carriage of a spark the most that ever I saw any man have.'

The detailed record of his playgoing ends inevitably with the cessation of his journal, but he evidently did not lose his love of the theatre. In the early months of 1680 he briefly resumed his daily record, in longhand and mainly as a political pre-caution. In those few weeks he saw Sir George Etherege's *She Would If She Could*, Thomas Otway's new tragedy *The Orphan, or The Unhappy Marriage*, and two other plays.

Music touched him even more than the drama. Had the *Diary* continued all his *Music* life we should have known his response to that great upsurge of English music associated with the name of Purcell. Henry Purcell senior, father or possibly uncle

Like the unknown in the picture, Pepys often played the lute alone in his room

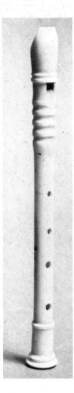

of the future composer, he had known in his early days in Axe Yard, and the forward-looking Matthew Locke, who wrote music for Charles's coronation procession. At a crisis in his public life in 1679, and actually under arrest, he asked for the music of John Blow's latest anthem.

'Music is the thing of the world I love most,' he once declared, and again in a lighter, but no less sincere, mood: 'Music and women I cannot but give way to, whatever my business is.' He sang with his friends – as the spontaneous old English custom was – in tavern and coffee house, at home and at sea. He sang equally, just as he played his lute or flageolet or bass viol, in the solitude of his room for the pure joy of it. A good singing voice or the ability to play the harpsichord was a strong recommendation when engaging a servant. At the suggestion of his friend, Thomas Hill, a music-loving merchant who had gone out to Portugal, he took into his household for several years a gifted young man from Lisbon named Cesare Morelli, with a fine singing voice trained in Rome, and other qualifications, secretarial as well as musical. However, Morelli's Catholicism proved a dangerous embarrassment when intolerance mounted in 1678.

Pepys had earlier taken a few lessons in composition and was able, with immense satisfaction, to set down a song or two of his own making, 'Gaze not on swans' and 'Beauty retire', the latter to some lines from Davenant's *Siege of Rhodes*. Not least of the varied pleasures Mrs Knipp gave him was her rendering of this. 'A very fine song it seems to be,' he noted complacently.

(*Opposite*) The flageolet was
only one of Pepys's instruments

Cesare Morelli's music book:
young Morelli spent several
years in the Pepys household,
combining secretarial duties
with musical instruction

The proud composer with
the manuscript of 'Beauty
retire': 'A very fine song it
seems to be'

(*Below*) 'Beauty retire', Pepys's
setting of Davenant's lines

As the years went by and his eyesight deteriorated, music became more and more the art he could enjoy. Reading was difficult, as was writing, and the literary projects he conceived at different times, such as a biography of my Lord and a history of the Navy, were destined to remain unrealized. He liked paintings up to a point – his taste was for the realistic and to him almost the highest achievement was a successful *trompe-l'œil* – and he collected prints, but worsening vision could only diminish his pleasure in them. Music, fortunately, which had always provided him with his deepest aesthetic experience, never failed him to the end.

The Royal Society   There was something shallower about his interest in science, or 'philosophy' as it was then called, though he was drawn to dabble in it by his omnivorous curiosity. His was the age in which science was emerging from the mists of alchemy, astrology and dogmatic devotion to the ancients. Experiment was in the air. Through the troubled years of Civil War and Commonwealth lively minds had been in contact through an 'Invisible College'. On 28 November 1660 a dozen gentlemen assembled in an actual college, the former home of an Elizabethan merchant, Sir Thomas Gresham, in Bishopsgate Street, which he had endowed for daily lectures. On this occasion the lecturer was the young Professor Wren, who had not yet

A Dutch interior, with a hint of that *trompe-l'œil* quality which the diarist so much admired

turned his mind to architecture. The group agreed to meet every Wednesday at three o'clock and pay a shilling each. Pepys was not the man to be left out of anything so interesting, and by 23 January 1661 he was recording his first visit to Gresham College, when the company included John Evelyn, William Petty, the statistician and political economist, and that romantic blend of intellectual and adventurer, Sir Kenelm Digby.

The King himself, who collected clocks, experimented with herbs from his own physic garden, and had a chemistry laboratory in his private apartments, joined the group some months later, granted the charter which formally constituted the Royal Society, and gave a silver gilt mace to be carried before its president.

At these Wednesday gatherings Pepys watched experiments, heard lectures and mingled freely with the outstanding scientists of the day. There was Robert Boyle, pioneer of modern chemistry. There was Robert Hooke, with his wonderful drawings done with the aid of his improved microscope, inventor too of air pumps, barometers, spirit levels and countless other devices. There was Dr John Wilkins, later a bishop, who as far back as 1638 had written *The Discovery of a World in the Moon*, adding a prophetically entitled appendix, *The Possibility of a Passage Thither*.

(*Right above*) The Royal Society mace, presented by Charles II

Robert Hooke's microscope

Hooke's drawing of a flea under the microscope

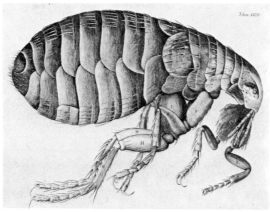

Pepys's intial interest may have flagged, or he may have found some of these speculative discussions above his head, or perhaps he could not spare the time. By November 1666, he had so far dropped out that he did not know that the meetings were being held, but he listened with interest to a description, by one of the active members, of an experiment in blood-transfusion between two dogs. 'If it takes,' Dr Croone told him, 'it may be of mighty use to man's health.'

It was John Evelyn, who became Secretary of the Royal Society in 1672, who begged Pepys to come back in 1680. The Society was in low water, its very survival in question, and Pepys, by then an eminent public figure and an experienced man of affairs, was just the person to put things right. 'I do assure you,' wrote Evelyn, 'we shall want one of your courage and address. . . . You know we do not usually fall on business till pretty late in expectation of a fuller company, and therefore if you decently could fall in amongst us by 6 or 7, it would, I am sure, infinitely oblige . . . the whole Society.'

He did not plead in vain. The Society picked up. Two years later it could afford to make a new rule for a stricter consideration of candidates, 'as whether they would really be useful', and more control on the admission of the honorary members. In 1684 Pepys, very much the amateur in scientific matters but the professional in administration, was rewarded with the Presidency, and in that capacity he gave his blessing to Newton's *Principia* when it was published. So in the end, though science never engaged his passionate interest as did music and the other arts, it is arguable that his service to science was of the greater lasting significance.

Such eminence would have seemed a far-off dream to Pepys when, in the early 1660's, he attended those early meetings at Gresham College. Other ambitions concerned him more. He lay in bed with Elizabeth discussing when they would be able to afford their own coach and whether some day he might achieve a knight-hood. But there were other times, too, when he dared not look further ahead than the next morning.

On 7 June 1665 he wrote, 'I did in Drury Lane see two or three houses marked with a red cross upon the doors, and "Lord have mercy upon us" writ there; which was a sad sight to me, being the first of the kind that, to my remembrance, I ever saw.'

London had for seventeen years been remarkably free of the plague which for centuries had recurred at varying intervals and with varying severity. Now, however, the city, with many other parts of England, suffered a final onslaught of dreadful intensity. Week by week the death roll in the capital mounted. By the end of June a mass exodus was in progress. King and Court fled, and after several moves settled in Oxford. Government departments were evacuated to various places. The Exchequer was removed to the fantastical, now obliterated Tudor palace of Nonsuch, whither Pepys had to ride more than once on business.

A hand-bell to give notice of the approaching plague-carts with their loads of dead

72

Sir Isaac Newton, elected a Fellow of the Royal Society in 1672 and President from 1703, being re-elected annually until his death in 1727. Newton's classic *Principia*, published with Pepys's authority as President of the Royal Society

He himself, alone of the Navy Board, remained in London, though he sent Elizabeth to the relative safety of Woolwich. He was mortally afraid, every day he was appalled by the sights he saw and the accounts he heard, and he made his will in the knowledge that his own turn might come at any time. But there was pressing work to be done and he would not neglect it. War had been declared against the Dutch and the fleet had to be maintained at sea. On the very day after noting those sinister crosses in Drury Lane he received news of a great naval victory. The Duke of York had himself commanded as High Admiral, and Sandwich had distinguished himself. The war continued. Another success was scored when my Lord captured a rich Dutch convoy from the East Indies and brought his prizes to the Nore, but the distribution of the plunder provoked scandal and controversy, and added greatly to Pepys's worries. There was trouble, too, with contractors and victuallers, and the very seamen who had won these victories could obtain no pay. Pepys's warm heart was moved by their plight. 'The great burden we have upon us at this time at the office, is the providing for prisoners and

The Plague

73

Multituds flying from London by water in boats & barges

Flying by land

Burying the dead with a bell before them.   Searchers.

Carts full of dead to bury.

Nonsuch, Henry VIII's fantastical palace
in Surrey: Charles gave it to his mistress,
Lady Castlemaine, in 1670, but she
never lived there and eventually sold it
off for demolition and property
development

(Left) The Great Plague of 1665
The Plague caused a general exodus of
government departments. For his
business with the Exchequer Pepys had
to ride out to Nonsuch

By the King.
A PROCLAMATION
For removing the Receipt of His Majesties Exchequer from
Westminster to *Nonsuch.*

CHARLES R.

The Kings most Excellent Majesty taking into his Princely Consideration the great and dangerous increase of the Plague in and about the City of Westminster, where his Majesties Receipt of Exchequer hath been hitherto kept; & willing, as much as is possible, to prevent the further danger which might ensue as well to his own Officers, which are necessarily to attend the same Receipt, as to other his loving Subjects, who shall have occasion either for Receipt or Payment of Moneys to repair thither; hath therefore taken Order for the present Remove of the Receipt of his said Exchequer, together with the Tally-Office, and all things thereunto belonging, from thence to his Majesties Honour of Nonsuch in the County of Surrey: And hath thought fit by this his Proclamation to Publish, That the same shall be there opened on the Fifteenth day of August next, to the end that all persons whom the same may concern, may take notice whither to repair upon all occasions, concerning the bringing in, or issuing out of his Majesties Treasure at the Receipt of his Exchequer. Willing and requiring all Sheriffs, Bayliffs, Collectors, and all other Officers, Accomptants, and persons whatsoever, who are to pay in any Moneys into the said Receipt of his Majesties Exchequer, or otherwise to attend the same, to keep their Days and times at Nonsuch aforesaid, and there to do, pay, and perform in all things, as they should, or ought to have done at Westminster, if the said Receipt of Exchequer had continued there. And this to be done and observed until His Majesty shall publish and declare his further pleasure to the contrary.

Given at Our Court at *Hampton-Court*, the Six and twentieth day of *July*, 1665. in the Seventeenth year of Our Reign.

God save the King.

LONDON,
Printed by *John Bill* and *Christopher Barker*, Printers to the Kings most
Excellent Majesty, 1665.

The royal palace at East Greenwich, where the Navy Office removed during the Plague

sick men that are recovered, they lying before our office doors all night and all day, poor wretches. Having been on shore, the Captains won't receive them on board, and other ships we have not to put them on, nor money to pay them off, or provide for them. God remove this difficulty!'

The Navy Office had by this time been ordered to move down-river to Green-wich, so that he was able to spend the night quite often with Elizabeth at her Woolwich lodgings two or three miles away. Walking to and fro on those September days he timed himself, 'my minute watch in my hand', and it pleased his methodical mind to see how closely each quarter of an hour brought him to the same stage on his road. Otherwise, there was little enough routine in that hectic summer and autumn of 1665. He was constantly on the move – back into the stricken city on necessary errands, down to the Nore to confer with my Lord, to Chatham dockyard and Rochester, even to a country-house week-end in Essex for the wedding of Sandwich's daughter to Carteret's son. It was typical of his sanguine temperament that, despite the ever-present shadow of the plague (nearly 70,000 people died in London alone) and the worries of his office ('Want of money in the Navy puts every thing out of order. Men grow mutinous; and nobody here to mind the business of the Navy but myself'), he looked back on that period as a remarkably happy one. He was doing his duty, and, after that, he was enjoying

Lady Castlemaine, later Duchess of Cleveland: a royal mistress whose very laundry, hung out to dry in the Privy Gardens at Whitehall, filled Pepys with a strange excitement. (*Right*) Frances Stewart in 1664 – aged 17, and the King's mistress for a year past. Pepys noted her, 'with her sweet eye' and 'little Roman nose . . . the greatest beauty I ever saw'

life, his enjoyment doubtless sharpened by his awareness of mortality. 'Much mirth,' says the *Diary*. 'To supper very merry. . . . Mighty merry . . . I did laugh till I was ready to burst.' Such entries are numerous. But he was thankful when the colder weather brought the pestilence to an end, and he was able to resume life in his own home with Elizabeth.

Even the King, briefed by his brother, realized how much the Navy owed to its zealous Clerk. At Hampton Court, that January, he went up to him and said, 'Mr Pepys, I do give you thanks for your good service all this year, and I assure you I am very sensible of it.'

Such soft words were gratifying, but some hard cash for the necessities of the service would have been welcome too. 'God knows what will become of all the King's matters in a little time,' Pepys had written gloomily some months earlier, 'for he runs in debt every day.' Charles seemed to care for nothing but his mistresses. 'The King do spend most of his time in feeling and kissing them naked. . . . But this lechery will never leave him.'

'I did see the houses at that end of the bridge all on fire . . . which did trouble me for poor little Michell and our Sarah on the bridge.' *Diary*, 2 Sept. 1666

The Great Fire The monarch did display some real concern for his subjects in the Great Fire, the following September. Pepys was called to the window at three o'clock in the morning by one of his maids, but the red glow was distant and he went back to sleep without unduly worrying. He rose late, it being Sunday, and thought no more of the fire till the same maid came to tell him that it had destroyed three hundred houses and was still raging. He then hurried out to investigate for himself, visiting the Lieutenant of the Tower near by, and taking a boat to get a general picture of the situation from the river. Appalled by the extent of the fire, and the absence of any organized attempt to combat it, he had himself rowed up to Whitehall, where he was quickly called into the King's presence, and 'did tell the King and Duke of York what I saw, and that unless his Majesty did command houses to be pulled down nothing could stop the fire.' Charles accepted the suggestion and told him to convey it, as a royal command, to the Lord Mayor. The Duke of York added an offer of troops if required, and Pepys hurried back into the City, where he found an exhausted Lord Mayor, 'like a fainting woman', and delivered his message.

In the afternoon he joined the King and the Duke in the royal barge. The demolitions were being carried out, but a wind was fanning the flames and the fire was advancing too rapidly to be halted. That evening he feared for his own home and the office next door. He prepared his most important papers for removal, along with his money, for as was customary in those times he kept it at home, in bags of gold, and he now had some thousands of pounds. Most of his household goods were carried out into the garden, 'it being brave dry, and moonshine, and warm weather'.

78

His neighbours, the Battens, had already ordered carts from the country. They lent him one to take his money, plate and most valuable possessions to a house in Bethnal Green, and at four o'clock in the morning he set off, riding on the cart in his dressing-gown. Neither he nor Elizabeth had any sleep that night.

For the next two days they worked tirelessly, struggling to get their bulky chattels down to a wharf near the Tower where they could be put aboard a lighter. Penn dug a pit in his garden to bury his wine. Pepys followed his example, adding office papers he could not otherwise dispose of, together with Parmesan cheese. He and Elizabeth subsisted on the cold remnants of the Sunday dinner, their last normal meal, and snatched what sleep they could on a quilt belonging to Hewer, the young clerk.

The Duke of York visited the office – he was riding up and down in the City with his bodyguard, doing what he could to restrain panic and looting. Pepys's respect for James II is understandable. Whatever his shortcomings, James was a conscientious naval man, and it was mainly in this context that Pepys had dealings with him. He came to the office again the next day. Pepys missed him, but wrote a hasty note, requesting his authority to 'pull down houses, rather than lose this office, which would much hinder the King's business'. For this work he suggested summoning all the dockyard workers from Woolwich and Deptford. That evening an even more drastic remedy was applied – the blowing up of houses with gunpowder, which he saw done in the next street most effectively.

The flight from the burning city

Cathedral of S. Paul

Before and after the Fire. The shell of St Paul's remained as the outstanding landmark

In the end, though the fire reached the corner of Seething Lane, his house and office escaped. They were left on the edge of a charred wilderness stretching westwards to Temple Bar. The City of his childhood had gone – over thirteen thousand houses, including his father's, along with St Paul's, Guildhall, Exchange, and countless churches, taverns, shops and coffee houses. His word-picture of those terrible days and their aftermath contrasts with his friend Evelyn's more literary account. Evelyn quotes Latin and recalls the fate of Troy. The reader of Pepys almost smells his fear along with the smoke, feels the hot rubble scorching his shoes, and shares his resentment at being charged, in this emergency, twopence for 'a plain penny loaf'.

The devastation of the Fire. Seething Lane, north-west of the Tower, had the narrowest of escapes

The 'Four Days' Fight', 1666, in which De Ruyter beat Albemarle

Medway disaster   One national catastrophe followed another. The Dutch war went badly. Just before the Fire, Albemarle had lost twenty warships in the 'Four Days' Fight' against De Ruyter. The Navy Office could get no money. Pepys thought of resigning, but he struggled on. Parliament was in session, demanding explanations. He faced its committees, and being essentially an honest and conscientious official with the facts and figures at his command, came well out of the ordeal. He got some money voted, but not enough to keep a battle fleet at sea. It had to be laid up ignominiously in the Medway behind a defensive boom. Then came the crowning humiliation, when De Ruyter sailed in, broke the boom, and destroyed the English fleet. There was panic in London, invasion or revolution expected. The storm was weathered and peace made. Pepys feared lest his royal masters should make him a scapegoat, 'though, God knows! I have, in my own person, done my full duty. . . .' But when, after a sleepless night, he had to stand at the bar of the House of Commons and defend the conduct of the Navy Office before a crowded assembly, he spoke confidently and fluently for three hours and received the warmest congratulations on all sides, even from the King himself.

82

De Ruyter, the Dutch admiral who humiliated the Navy in the Medway. (*Below*) The burning of the English warships in the Medway disaster of 1667

St Olave's Church, Hart Street, where Pepys and his wife were buried. A new gallery was specially added to accommodate the Navy Board, their households and staff

Married life   In those anxious early hours beforehand he had wakened Elizabeth to talk to him and give him comfort. Their odd, uneasy, sometimes cat-and-dog marriage had wonderfully survived the testing of twelve eventful years. It remained childless – sadly, for frequent *Diary* references testify to his kindly interest in boys and girls. One of his more disreputable London relatives, Uncle Wight, a fishmonger, suggested to Elizabeth that he should supply the child her husband could not. Whether in fact the deficiency was Pepys's cannot now be determined. Certainly, despite his numerous lapses with other women, there is no evidence that he ever fathered a child, though more than once he suffered temporary alarms.

    Most of the *Diary* entries suggest that his timidity prevented his going to all lengths. Using a transparent jumble of foreign words to cover what was already hidden in shorthand, he noted his encounter with a young woman who asked him not to send her husband to sea, when he 'pouvait avoir done any cose cum elle, but I did nothing, si ni baisser her'. Sometimes he carried familiarity a good deal further than that – he might record complacently, 'nulla puella negat', without specifying how much he demanded from the girl who denied nothing. It was certainly no Casanova who found time to chronicle such schoolboy trivialities as this flirtation during a church service: 'stood by a pretty modest maid, whom I did labour to take by the hand; but she would not, but got further and further from me; and at last, I could perceive her to take pins from her pockets to prick me if I should touch her again – which, seeing, I did forbear, and was glad I did spy her design. And then I fell to gaze upon another pretty maid, in a pew close to me . . . and I did go about to take her by the hand, which she suffered a little, and then withdrew. So the sermon ended . . . and my amours ended also.' At that date he was thirty-four years old.

In the autumn of 1668 there was a more serious affair, under his own roof, with a too attractive young maid, Deb Willett. Elizabeth discovered this and violent scenes followed. Deb departed, Samuel remained, and so did the battle-scarred marriage.

Pepys's eyesight had been troubling him for some time. Not only the many hours' poring over handwritten documents and accounts but even the candles in the playhouse 'did almost kill' him. He was convinced that he was going blind. Certainly he must give up, with extreme reluctance, a journal whose keeping imposed the extra strain of shorthand to preserve its secrets. So, on 31 May 1669, he *Diary closed* made the final entry, 'being not able to do it any longer, having done now so long as to undo my eyes almost every time that I take a pen in my hand. . . . And so I

Pepys's prayer book. In church, his eyes were apt to stray elsewhere

May

May. 31. 1669.

'Being not able to do it any
longer . . .': the final entry in the
Diary, foretelling blindness

The Pont Neuf, as Pepys and his
wife saw it on their visit
in 1669

Elizabeth's memorial
in St Olave's

betake myself to that course, which is almost as much as to see myself go into my grave: for which, and all the discomforts that will accompany my being blind, the good God prepare me!'

His fears proved baseless. But he did not feel able to resume the confidential daily record he had kept for almost a decade, and thereafter his life, though richly documented, lacks the confessional intimacy of the 1660's.

Soon after closing his journal he embarked with Elizabeth on their long-deferred visit to France and Holland. Pepys had always delighted in talk of foreign parts – he would listen for hours to his friends' accounts of the singing in Rome or the odd manners of the Muscovites, but his own chances to travel were all too few. Now he made the most of those two months, visiting Paris and other cities. In Brussels Elizabeth fell ill. She struggled home, collapsed with a fever, and died on 10 November. She was still only twenty-nine. Pepys was thirty-six.

Death of Elizabeth

Remarkably, in that age of early bereavements and remarriages, and in view of his strong sexuality, he never took a second wife. Nor, with the discontinuance of his journal, is there any evidence of irregular affairs. At one stage he was power-fully attracted to Mary Skinner, the witty daughter of a merchant in the next street. She returned his affection, but for some reason her family broke off their friendship with Pepys and nothing came of it. Mary never married, and more than twenty years later – twenty years during which he lived the typical life of a prosperous and

87

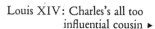
Louis XIV: Charles's all too influential cousin ►

Charles II, at the time of granting the Hudson's Bay Company its charter in 1670

respectable widower, employing the more or less unsatisfactory housekeepers found for him by his women friends – she moved in and ran his home. Her precise status is uncertain, but no scandal is recorded.

Work for the Navy   In his undoubted grief at the loss of his sometimes irritating but always beloved Elizabeth, Pepys found distraction in his work. He had come back from his foreign holiday to meet a crisis in the affairs of the Navy Office. Its Parliamentary critics were in full cry again. Hardly was Elizabeth in her grave than he had to concentrate on preparing the thoroughly documented answer which no one else in the department was competent to give. He did the work, as he did all his work for another twenty years of devoted public service, with the help of trustworthy clerks who read aloud and wrote at his dictation. If his eyes were useless for close work, his memory and mental capacity for marshalling figures and arguments were un' impaired. Thanks to those qualities he was able to confute the critics with fifty folio pages of detailed and unanswerable justification. The King, at last bestirring himself and displaying an intelligent interest which surprised Pepys, presided over the inquiry in person and made no secret of his sympathy.

Having defended the past as best he could, Pepys had his hands full preparing for the new war with the Dutch which the Treaty of Dover, made by Charles with his royal cousin of France, now rendered inevitable. The treaty embodied a cynical

A Dutch artist's impression of Windsor, where Pepys had occasionally to wait upon the King

Plymouth in 1673: Pepys sailed there in the royal yacht with Charles

In Oxford Pepys paid ten shillings to view the Sheldonian Theatre, new built by his friend Christopher Wren

scheme under which the French, with English naval assistance, were to invade the Netherlands and partition the country, leaving only a small part nominally independent but in fact a French satellite state, with William of Orange (whose character was sadly misjudged by the optimistic schemers) ruling it as Louis's puppet. The secret clauses of the treaty, known only to the Catholics among Charles's advisers, brought French gold, not enough, but welcome in so far as it removed the King's dependence on Parliament. Pepys, with inadequate funds, had to equip a fleet for the anti-Dutch alliance. He travelled widely, waiting on the King at Windsor and Newmarket, sailing with him in his yacht from Portsmouth to Plymouth, surveying the timber resources of the Forest of Dean, visiting the nearby ironworks, and sightseeing *en route*. Fortunately his distant vision remained good. He could appreciate the architecture of the new Sheldonian Theatre at Oxford and the pastoral scenery of the Cotswolds.

Battle of Sole Bay, 1672: Pepys lost his cousin and life-long ally when 'my Lord' was blown up in his flagship, the *Royal James*

War came in 1672, and for England lasted until 1674, bringing none of the easy success that had been hoped for. With the Duke of York on active service at sea, Pepys found a new and rather trying chief in Prince Rupert. On 28 May the Duke, with Sandwich as his second-in-command, engaged the Dutch fleet in a tremendous but indecisive battle. Sandwich fought heroically and was blown up with his flagship. His body was recovered from the sea and he was given, as Vice-Admiral of England, a splendid funeral in Westminster Abbey, Pepys having an honoured place in the ceremony. Thus ended the long and loyal association of the two cousins. For years Pepys had been standing on his own feet – sometimes indeed more firmly in favour than 'my Lord' himself – but he never forgot the kinsman who had given him his chance.

'Chance without merit brought me in,' he had once confessed to his friend, the merchant Hill, 'and diligence only keeps me so, and will, living as I do among so many lazy people that the diligent man becomes necessary, that they cannot do anything without him.' Diligence continued to be his watchword.

nce Rupert: Pepys found him a trying
·erior during the Duke of York's absence
sea

The young widower: Pepys about 1670

It was not always quickly rewarded. Twice he was denied the advancement he coveted, when the posts of Comptroller and then of Secretary to the Lord High Admiral fell vacant. But in 1673 his moment came. The new Test Act made it impossible for the Duke of York, as a Roman Catholic, to continue in office. But, instead of appointing a Protestant, the King transferred the functions of Lord High Admiral to a fifteen-man commission. He chose Pepys for the key post of 'Secretary to the Office of Lord High Admiral of England', which finally confirmed him as the head of naval administration. Pepys moved up the last step, and his old functions as Clerk of the Acts were shared by his own brother, John, and his former assistant, Tom Hayter.

Promoted Secretary

Other honours and positions followed. He had long hankered after a seat in Parliament, had tried for one at Aldeburgh just before his wife's death, but had had no success in winning over the handful of burgesses who in those days selected the MP. Now, in November 1673, thanks to the local influence of the Earl of Norwich and despite the unfounded allegation that he was a 'Bluddy Papist', he

93

won the Norfolk seat of Castle Rising by twenty-nine votes to seven. Within the next few years he became Master of Trinity House, Governor of Christ's Hospital, and Master of the Clothworkers' Company.

Early in 1673 his house and office, which had survived the Great Fire, were destroyed in a local conflagration along with about thirty other buildings. Temporary premises were found and Pepys himself stayed with his friend James Houblon, a merchant. Then, in his new capacity as Secretary to the Admiralty, he moved to Derby House in Cannon Row, which stood conveniently midway between Palace and Parliament, had elegant living quarters for himself, and possessed a sheltered garden in which he could plant orange trees.

For the next five years he was at the height of his career. He had power at last to attempt what needed to be done. He restored order to the formerly chaotic state of the Navy. Establishments were laid down, governing grades and numbers of men; duties were defined, and pay, discipline and service conditions generally improved. Thirty new vessels were built. And, with a seat in Parliament, he was able to explain and defend what was being done. If, sometimes, opponents accused him of being arrogant, it was because he knew what he was talking about, and knew too that often they did not. The very fullness of his knowledge made him speak at excessive length, while his great pride in the dignity of his office laid him open to the charge of being pompous. In private life he was not so. No man so rich in friendships could have been, and the character suggested in the *Diary* is not that of a man given to lengthy monologues but essentially that of a good listener.

Inevitably he made enemies, and in 1679 they found their opening. A new

Christ's Hospital, a royal charity school for orphans: Pepys became a governor in 1676

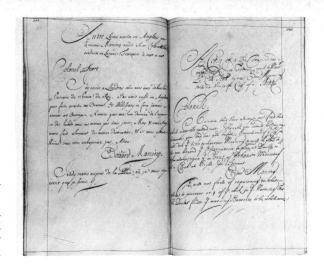

Evidence collected by Pepys for his defence: Colonel Scott was a remarkable scoundrel who gave false testimony against him

Parliament, in which he himself was elected as member for Harwich, came in on a wave of anti-Catholic, anti-French sentiment. Pepys's old loyalty to the Duke of York lent colour to the allegation that he too was a Papist. In the prevalent witch-hunting atmosphere he was hounded into resignation and sent to the Tower on a charge of selling naval secrets to the French. He was released on bail after six weeks and, having lost his official residence, went to live with his former clerk and friend, Will Hewer, in York Buildings at the bottom of Buckingham Street. There he spent almost a year collecting evidence and marshalling the kind of impregnable defence at which he excelled. It was never needed. After the usual agony of legal delays the charges against him were withdrawn.

Resignation

The Tower of London: Pepys spent six weeks there as a prisoner in 1679

Pepys missed shipwreck in the Duke of York's flagship sailing to Scotland, having just transferred for greater comfort to one of the accompanying yachts

His enemies, nevertheless, had scored a victory. He was out of office and remained so for most of the next four or five years, though he still enjoyed the regard of the royal brothers. In 1682 he sailed with the Duke to Scotland and had a narrow escape when the flagship was wrecked with the loss of two hundred lives. Happily Pepys had earlier transferred himself to one of the accompanying yachts, because the flagship was uncomfortably crowded. He spent a week independently touring in Scotland, seeing Glasgow, Stirling and Linlithgow as well as Edinburgh, and then sailed home at leisure, calling at Newcastle (where he was feasted by the Mayor and made a freeman), Durham and Hull.

Tangier   The next year he had a chance to travel further afield, when at the King's suggestion he was appointed secretary to Lord Dartmouth's expedition to Tangier. The secret purpose of this expedition, known only to Pepys and Dartmouth himself, was to arrange the evacuation of the base, a useless expense and untenable in the face of unfriendly Moors who controlled even its water supply.

Foul weather blew the fleet off course. For days Pepys was miserably sick. Altogether it was three weeks before his buckled shoes touched North African soil.

Then he was bitten to death by bugs, discomforted by the heat, and appalled by the immorality of the English colony, garrison and civilians alike, but especially the swashbuckling and licentious Governor, Colonel Kirke. Being Pepys, he could not fail to derive some pleasure and interest from this glimpse of a foreign land, but on the whole he did not enjoy his stay. His particular responsibility was to value the property of countless owners, English and Portuguese, and assess their claims for compensation. He set to work with his usual efficiency, and, though obstructed by the lethargy of the claimants, got the job done. The expedition had reached Tangier on 14 September. By 5 November all the civilians had left. A

Tangier before abandonment. Like Bombay (only less valuable) the port had come into British possession as the dowry of Catherine of Braganza. (*Below*) Tangier after demolition in 1683

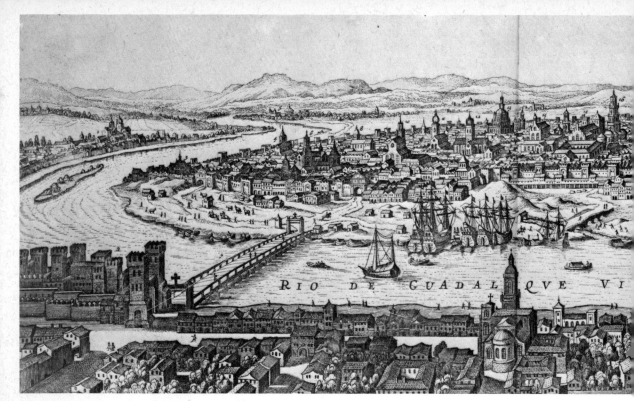

Seville, where Pepys and Hewer spent a week of dogged sightseeing, despite a continuous downpour, in January 1684. (*Right*) William Hewer, about 1685: assistant, life-long friend and

month later, his work finished, Pepys crossed to Spain with Will Hewer for a well-earned holiday. Heavy rains and floods curtailed their travelling, and they spent most of their ten weeks in Seville and Cadiz before rejoining Dartmouth for the homeward voyage.

Return to Office   Charles was now near the end of his reign, ruling independently of Parliament. He felt free to abolish the Admiralty Commission set up five years before. Pepys was called to Windsor and given the new post of Secretary for Admiralty Affairs, with an increased salary of £2,000 – and no master but the King. He was supreme, so much so that, preferring to stay in Buckingham Street, he took over the whole building from Hewer and transferred the staff from Derby House. There he remained – narrowly escaping yet another disastrous fire – until the beginning of 1688 when he moved from No. 12 to No. 14, a splendid new mansion at the bottom of the street, overlooking the Thames.

These were the years of his greatest glory. He saw the King regularly, and the Duke who succeeded as James II in 1685, and had – deservedly – the confidence of both. He needed it. In his years in the wilderness all his reforms had gone by the board. The Navy was run down, discipline poor, commands taken from the

98

companion in Pepys's last days. (*Below*) Letter Patent, appointing Pepys to the new-made post of 'Secretary of and for the Affairs and businesses of and concerning our Admiralty of England'

James, Duke of York, with his first wife, Anne Hyde, and their daughters, the future Queens, Mary II and Anne

experienced captains (the 'tarpaulins') and given to gentlemen amateurs. All was to do again. Indefatigably Pepys set to work. In everything he spoke in the King's name and no one dared to challenge him.

The accession of James, that sincere enthusiast for the Navy, could only enhance the Secretary's influence. As a Baron of the Cinque Ports Pepys helped to carry the canopy over his old master's head in the Coronation procession, and was an honoured guest at the banquet afterwards. A few weeks later he was mustering frigates in an unsuccessful attempt to prevent the Duke of Monmouth's landing in the West Country. He had no sympathy with the hapless rebels. Untroubled by political or religious fervour on either side, he never wavered in his loyalty to the established order.

James knew it. Once, in a burst of private confidence, he told Pepys that his brother had died a Catholic, and backed the assertion by producing some papers arguing against the Church of England which, if not composed by Charles, were certainly in his handwriting. He even gave Pepys copies, authenticating them with his own signature.

The Duke of York, whose care for the Navy won Pepys's esteem, attains the throne as James II

James II's coronation: as a Baron of the Cinque Ports Pepys had a place of honour and responsibility, holding the nearer of the front poles supporting the canopy

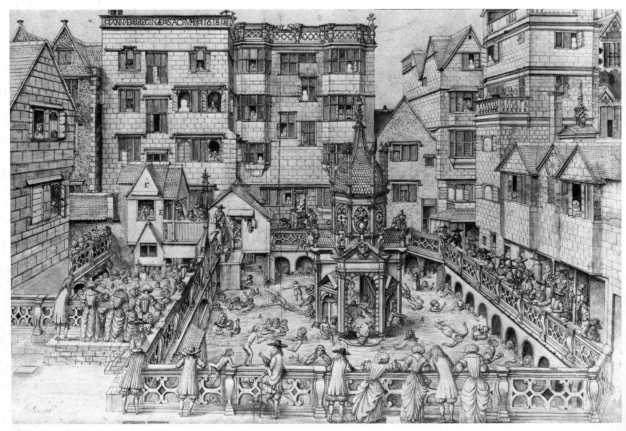

London, seen across the river from Horseferry, showing the dome of Wren's new St Paul's

Christopher Wren, whose designs changed the face of Pepys's childhood London, destroyed in the Fire. The men knew each other well

(*Left above*) Monmouth's Rebellion, 1685: Pepys failed to forestall it by naval blockade

(*Left below*) Bath, where Pepys was summoned to attend James II on his progress in the summer of 1687

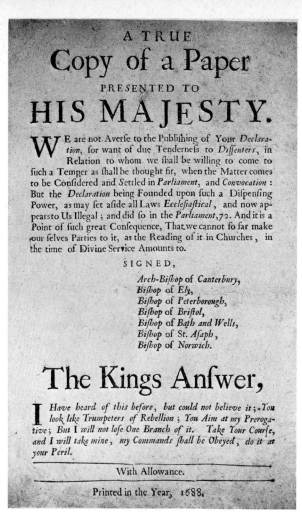

A TRUE Copy of a Paper PRESENTED TO HIS MAJESTY.

WE are not Averfe to the Publifhing of Your *Declaration*, for want of due Tendernefs to *Diffenters*, in Relation to whom we fhall be willing to come to fuch a Temper as fhall be thought fit, when the Matter comes to be Confidered and Settled in *Parliament*, and *Convocation* : But the *Declaration* being Founded upon fuch a Difpenfing Power, as may fet afide all Laws *Ecclefiaftical*, and now appears to Us Illegal ; and did fo in the *Parliament*, 72. And it is a Point of fuch great Confequence, That we cannot fo far make our felves Parties to it, as the Reading of it in Churches, in the time of Divine Service Amounts to.

SIGNED,

Arch-Bifhop of *Canterbury*,
Bifhop of *Ely*,
Bifhop of *Peterborough*,
Bifhop of *Briftol*,
Bifhop of *Bath and Wells*,
Bifhop of *St. Afaph*,
Bifhop of *Norwich*.

The Kings Anfwer,

I Have heard of this before, but could not believe it ; You look like Trumpeters of Rebellion ; You Aim at my Prerogative ; But I will not lofe One Branch of it. Take Your Courfe, and I will take mine, my Commands fhall be Obeyed, do it at your Peril.

With Allowance.

Printed in the Year, 1688.

The King's clash with the Seven Bishops: a contemporary broadside circulated in a summer of political crisis

William of Orange in 1686

So, for three years, Pepys flourished as never before. Honourable positions – though curiously enough no title – were pressed upon him. President of the Royal Society, Master of Trinity House, Deputy Lieutenant for Huntingdonshire, MP for Harwich, he blossomed as a patron of the arts, a collector, a giver of concerts in his stately house beside the Thames. He was rich. 'Money, which sweetens all things,' he had noted long ago. He was not to be swayed in decisions against the King's interests, but it would never have occurred to him to refuse the perquisites that fell harmlessly into his lap.

All this ended with the Glorious Revolution. At the historic trial of the seven bishops, whom James insisted on prosecuting for 'seditious libel' for their petition

104

The Seven Bishops leaving the Tower

against his Declaration of Indulgence admitting Catholics to civil and military appointments, Pepys gave brief, impartial evidence, unmoved either by his regard for the King or by the Protestant mob howling at the witnesses as they entered and left the court. By late August an invasion by William of Orange seemed likely. Pepys stopped all naval leave and mobilized the fleet, which mustered at the Nore under Lord Dartmouth's command. An anxious month or two followed, while contrary winds held the Dutch fleet in port and Pepys strove tactfully but vainly to activate his over-cautious admiral. Then the weather changed. The 'Protestant wind' blew from the east. On 5 November Pepys learnt that William had sailed through the Dover straits the previous day.

A medal struck to celebrate the acquittal of the Seven Bishops

Cavalier's ivory medallion, 1688, of Pepys at the zenith of his career

William of Orange arrives in London, 28 January 1689

The next evening brought news of his landing in Devon. James is said to have been sitting for his portrait by Kneller, as a royal admiral, when the dispatch was handed to him by a lieutenant from the frigate *Swallow*. He read it and dropped it on the floor. 'I have promised Mr Pepys my picture,' he said, and the sitting continued.

Through no fault of Pepys, the Navy had failed in its primary duty of interception. The Secretary continued busily at his desk, but the main issue was now in other hands. William must be defeated on land. The King proposed to lead his own troops to the West Country. Pepys witnessed his will and attended him on the first day's march as far as Windsor. Then he went back to his own duties at the Admiralty, where, as the situation deteriorated day by day, he was soon concerned with an abortive plan to ship the infant Prince of Wales to safety in France. Soon the King, as his supporters melted away, saw the hopelessness of armed resistance and returned to London. Early one dark December morning Pepys was awakened to receive one of the royal pages with the message that James had fled.

Pepys's inexorable marshalling of detail, as shown in his *Memoires of the Royal Navy*

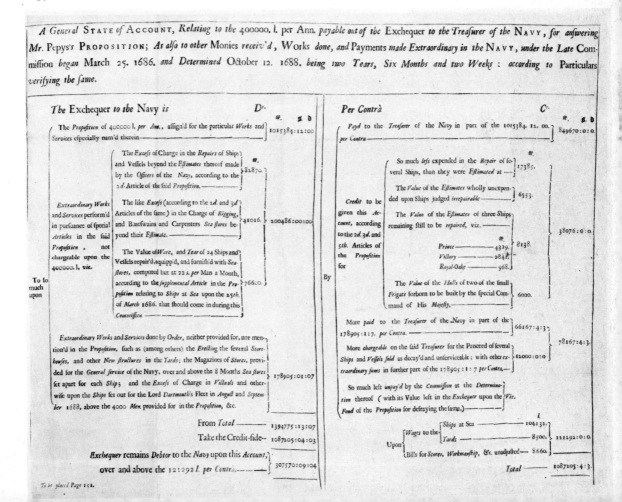

Pepys, for all his long connection with the King, had been in no way involved and he was not compromised. As a public servant he now behaved correctly, taking his instructions first from the provisional government set up under the Archbishop of Canterbury and then from the Prince of Orange, who summoned him to an audience on 19 December. For the time being all public servants were to remain in office and carry on their duties. Pepys did so with great dignity, never for one moment relaxing his authority though he guessed that his career was at an end. In the January elections for a new Parliament he lost his seat at Harwich. In February it was announced that all public servants should vacate their posts and be either replaced or reappointed. Pepys was not going to crawl to the new regime. He cleared his desk and sought no one's favour to keep it. Nominally, at least, his retirement was voluntary. As Evelyn fairly put it in his own private diary, 'When James II went out of England, he laid down his office, and would serve no more.'

Retirement

His enemies could not resist a final kick. In June 1690 he was arrested 'on suspicion of being affected to King James', but he was released on bail a few days later and the charges withdrawn in October. The conferment of the freedom of the City in 1699 sufficiently indicates that he remained a popular and respected figure.

Little drama disturbed those closing years, except for an encounter with masked highwaymen on Michaelmas Day 1693, when he was driving in his coach to Chelsea with his favourite nephew, John Jackson, his sister's son, and a party of ladies. With a pistol at his chest, Pepys surrendered his money and valuables, which characteristically included a silver ruler, a gold pencil, a magnifying glass, and five mathematical instruments, but he retained his dignity and persuaded the miscreants 'to be civil to the ladies and not to affright them'. Later, he gave evidence against the men at the Old Bailey and they were both sentenced to death.

His quiet retirement was cheered by the devotion of Mary Skinner, whom he called on his death-bed his 'dear child', leaving her a substantial legacy with 'the most full and lasting acknowledgment of my esteem, respect and gratitude to the Excellent Lady Mrs Mary Skinner for the many important effects of her steady friendship and assistances during . . . the last thirty-three years.' No less devoted was Will Hewer, who had himself prospered greatly, and had always a welcome for his old chief at his fine country house at Clapham. Pepys often stayed there, and made it his permanent home after his health began to break down in the summer of 1701.

Until then, he kept his own house by the water gate at the foot of Buckingham Street, entertaining his numerous friends, enjoying music, and arranging his books in their tall oak cases. His old passion for order and method never left him. The catalogue he made in 1693 reveals him as a pioneer of library system. He went on collecting. In 1698 he sent John Jackson on a tour of Italy and Spain to buy books and prints for him. His final catalogue in 1700 listed 2,474 volumes. By his death

John Jackson,
helpful nephew and heir

Pepys's library
in Buckingham Street

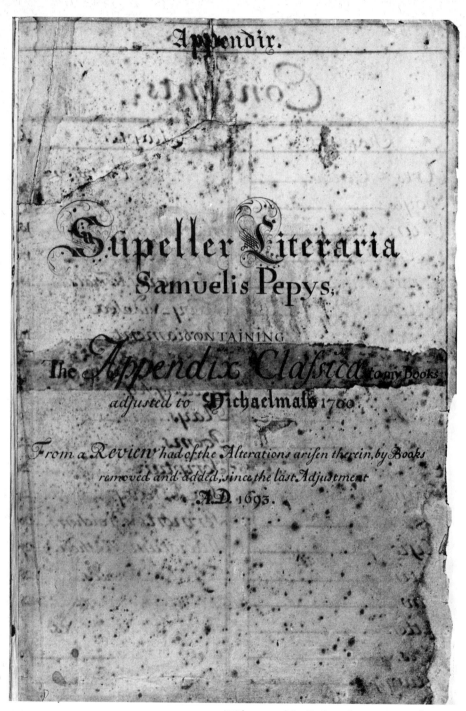

Title-page of the final catalogue, 1700, still in use

*Contents of my Collection (Nº 2137.)
of Printed Votes & other Publick Papers
relating to the two Parliaments begun ~
One at Westminster October 1679, the othr
at Oxford March 168 $\frac{0}{1}$.*

Contents.

Contents.	Year.	Mo.	Day	Pag.
List of the Parliament begun .	1680	Oct.	21	.1
Kings Speech to both Houses.	do.	do.	do.	5
Votes of the House of Commons { From	do.	do.	do.	15
{ To.	do.	Nov.	22	61
Address of the Commons to his Maj.tie for remov=ing Sr. Geo. Jeffreys from all Publ. Offices.	do.	do.	do.	62
Votes of the House of Commons { From.	do.	do.	23	63
{ To.	do.	do.	25	69
Address of both Houses for a Day of Humiliacon with his Majties Answer.	do.	do.	26	71
Votes of the House of Commons.	do.	do.	do.	73
Address of Do.— for removing the Lord ~ Halifax from Court with his Majties. Answ.	do.	do.	do.	75
Articles of Impeachment agst. Edwd. Seymour. Esqr. w. ye Votes of the Commons upon ye same	do.	do.	do.	77
Votes of the House of Commons { From.	do.	do.	27	79
{ To.	do.	do.	29	81

A pioneer of library system, he liked to catalogue every item

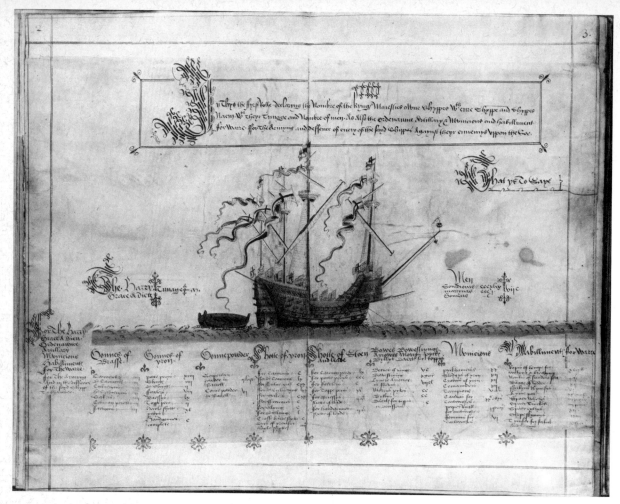

The *Great Harry*, from a folio
of parchment rolls, depicting
Henry VIII's navy,
which were given
to Pepys by Charles II

A page from the
'Monk's Drawing Book'

Pepys loved a beautiful binding: some of his books preserved in the library at Cambridge

Dr Thomas Gale, headmaster of St Paul's, who
married Pepys's cousin Barbara and was his friend

One of Pepys's treasures, a unique surviving copy of
Wynkyn de Worde's 'Introduction to the
Latin Tongue'

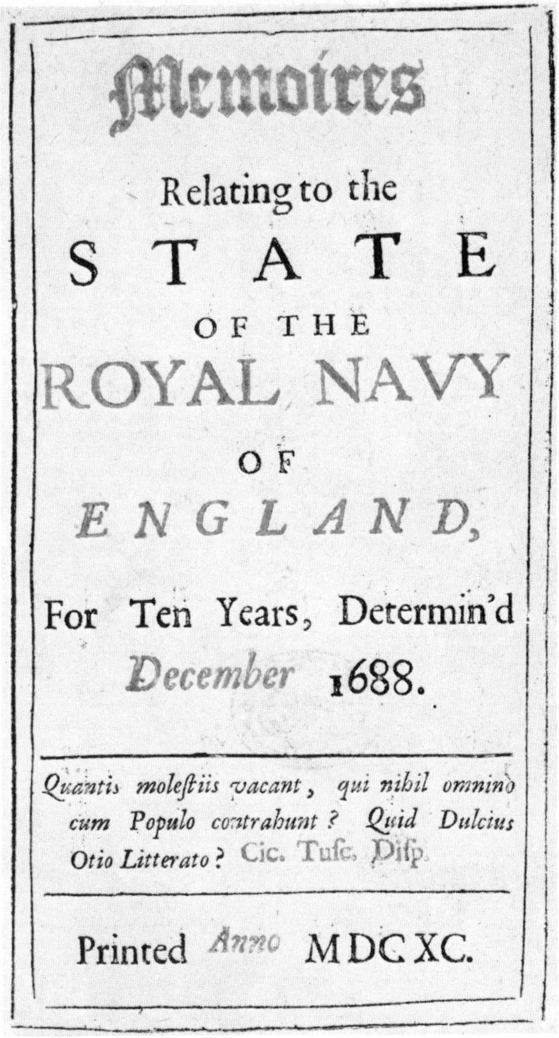

Memoires

Relating to the

S T A T E

OF THE

ROYAL NAVY

OF

ENGLAND,

For Ten Years, Determin'd
December 1688.

*Quantis molestiis vacant, qui nihil omninò
cum Populo contrahunt? Quid Dulcius
Otio Litterato?* Cic. Tusc. Disp.

Printed *Anno* MDCXC.

Title-page. His public career ended now (1690), Pepys could well quote Cicero, 'What sweeter than scholarly leisure?'

they had grown to 3,000. When his nephew died they passed with many of his papers and notebooks, including the journals which kept their secrets until deciphered and published (in part) in 1825, as the indivisible collection still treasured in the Pepys Library of his old college.

This collection includes sixty medieval manuscripts, some of music, and nearly two hundred early printed books dating back to Caxton and Wynkyn de Worde. The remarkable assembly of old ballads has almost a thousand unique items. Prints fill more than a dozen big albums. There are old plays, shorthand systems, engraved examples of calligraphy, and – invaluable to naval historians – the mass of research material gathered for the *magnum opus* he was never to complete. His sole published book was the *Memoires relating to the state of the Royal Navy 1679–1688*, printed in 1690.

SAMVEL PEPYS
born Feb^{ry} 25.1632.
died May 26.1703.

ERECTED·1883·BY·PVBLIC·SVBSCRIPTION·MAINLY·OWING
TO·THE·EFFORTS·OF·HENRY·BENJAMIN·WHEATLEY·1838-1917
D·C·L·F·S·A·EDITOR·OF·THE·COMPLETE·EDITION
OF·THE·DIARY·

John Evelyn, the other great diarist of the period, to whom Pepys was 'a particular friend for near forty years'

He was seventy when he died at Hewer's house in Clapham, after a lengthy *Death* illness, on 26 May 1703. He was buried, like Elizabeth, at St Olave's, close to the spot where they had spent so much of their tempestuous young married life together.

Evelyn, himself too ill to serve as a pall-bearer, summed up in his diary the man who had been his 'particular friend for near forty years'. He spoke of Pepys's 'great integrity' – 'a very worthy, industrious and curious person, none in England exceeding him in knowledge of the navy . . . universally beloved, hospitable, generous, learned in many things, skilled in music, a very great cherisher of learned men. . . .' It was not a bad epitaph, and in that age of hyperbolical eulogies it was better deserved than most.

Mens cujusque is est quisque

Pepys's appropriately nautical end-plate.
The no-less appropriate
Latin motto might be rendered
in Bacon's words, 'The mind is the man'

BIBLIOGRAPHICAL NOTE

The standard biography of Pepys is provided by Sir Arthur Bryant's three volumes, *Pepys: The Man in the Making, The Years of Peril* and *The Saviour of the Navy* (Cambridge University Press, 1933–38), an indispensable source which is here gratefully acknowledged. The best edition of the *Diary* is that edited by R. C. Latham and W. Matthews, publication of which was begun in 1970 by G. Bell & Son, superseding the same publisher's edition by H. B. Wheatley (1893–99), though the latter's supplementary volume, *Pepysiana*, retains its special value and interest. The only book Pepys himself published was his *Memoires relating to the state of the Royal Navy*, in 1690, a modern edition of which was edited by J. R. Tanner in 1906.

119

(*Left*) Pepys's Diary, with the handsome bindings in which he delighted

CHRONOLOGY

1633 Born on 23 February in London at Salisbury Court, fifth (and eldest survivor) of eleven children.

1642 Outbreak of Civil War. About this time he goes to live with Uncle Robert Pepys at Brampton and attends Huntingdon Grammar School.

1645 Returns home about this date and enters St Paul's School.

1649 Witnesses the execution of Charles I.

1650 Goes up to Magdalene College, Cambridge.

1653 Graduates B.A. in October and returns home.

1655 On 10 October marries Elizabeth le Marchant de St Michel, aged fifteen, daughter of an impoverished Huguenot. In this year, or at the beginning of the next, he enters the personal service of his influential cousin, Edward Mountagu, later Earl of Sandwich.

1658 About this time becomes a clerk in the Exchequer under George Downing.
26 March, operation for the stone.
Summer, takes a small house in Axe Yard.

3 September, Cromwell's death opens period of political unrest and uncertainty.

1659 In May Pepys sails to the Baltic on a brief mission to report to Mountagu.

1660 1 January, begins his *Diary*.
March, joins fleet as Mountagu's secretary.
May, sails to Holland to bring back Charles II.
July, appointed Clerk of the Acts and moves to a house in Seething Lane, next to the Navy Office.

1661 Witnesses Charles II's Coronation on 23 April.
Appointed a younger Brother of Trinity House and a Commissioner for Tangier. Attends one of the early meetings of the future Royal Society.

1665 Elected member of the Royal Society. Remains in London during first weeks of Plague, till the Navy Office is moved.

1666 2 September, outbreak of Great Fire. Pepys carries word to King and arranges for evacuation of the threatened Navy Office and his own house.

1667 Dutch burn the English fleet in the Medway.

1668 Pepys defends the naval administration in a much-praised three-hour speech at the bar of the House of Commons.

1669 31 May, closes *Diary* in expectation of going blind.
August–October, takes wife on tour to Paris and Brussels.
10 November, wife dies and is buried at St Olave's on the other side of Seething Lane.

1670 Pepys justifies the naval administration at a Parliamentary inquiry.
Secret clauses in the Treaty of Dover make the King (and the Navy) financially independent of Parliament. Pepys equips fleet to aid French against Dutch.

1672 Outbreak of Third Dutch War.
28 May, Mountagu (Earl of Sandwich) blown up in battle in his flagship.

1673 King promotes Pepys to be Secretary to the Office of Lord High Admiral of England, with an official residence at Derby House.
Pepys elected MP for Castle Rising.

1676 Master of Trinity House and Governor of Christ's Hospital.

1677 Master of the Clothworkers' Company.

1679 MP for Harwich.
Forced to resign from the Admiralty and sent to the Tower in March on charge of selling naval secrets to France. In July released on bail and goes to live with Will Hewer in Buckingham Street. Spends a year preparing his defence but the charge is dropped.

1682 Attends Duke of York on visit to Scotland.

1683 Sails to Tangier with Lord Dartmouth and helps to arrange evacuation of the base. Visits southern Spain with Will Hewer.

1684 Given new post of Secretary for Admiralty Affairs, moving the department to his house in Buckingham Street. December, becomes President of the Royal Society.

1685 6 February, Charles II dies and is succeeded by Duke of York as James II, at whose Coronation Pepys helps to carry the canopy.
Pepys is re-elected MP for Harwich.
Installed Master of Trinity House and Deputy Lieutenant of Huntingdonshire, and re-elected President of the Royal Society.

1687 Accompanies James on royal progress to Bath, Gloucester and Worcester.

1688 5 November, William of Orange lands in Devon. James flees abroad. Pepys continues the normal work of the Admiralty under the provisional government and then under the Prince.

1689 January, fails to secure re-election as MP. February, like all high officers of state he resigns his position but unlike others does not seek re-appointment and retires from public life.

1690 June, arrested on suspicion of Jacobite sympathies. Quickly released on bail. October, charges dropped.

1699 Freeman of City of London.

1701 About June, being in failing health, gives up Buckingham Street home and moves to Will Hewer's country house at Clapham.

1703 26 May, dies at Clapham. Buried at St Olave's.

LIST OF ILLUSTRATIONS

INDEX

Page numbers in italics refer to the illustrations